DARREN
THANK you for
Everything you do

714-624-2438

SECRETS REVEALED

THE NEXT BIG ASSET BREAKTHROUGH
EVERYTHING YOU NEED TO KNOW, BUT WERE AFRAID TO ASK

THE ULTIMATE METAMORPHOSIS OF:
NFT'S + QR + AR + GAMIFICATION

Andy Broadaway

Copyright © 2022 by Andy Broadaway. All rights reserved. No part of this publication may be reproduced, distributed, or transmitted in any form or by any means, including photocopying, recording, or other electronic or mechanical methods, without the prior written permission of the publisher, except in the case of brief quotations embodied in critical reviews and certain other noncommercial uses permitted by copyright law. For permission requests, write to the publisher, addressed "Attention: Permissions Coordinator," at: info@abundantpress.com.

Abundant Press www.AbundantPress.com
Ordering Information & Quantity Sales: Special discounts are available on quantity purchases by corporations, associations, and others. For details, contact the publisher. Orders by U.S. & International trade bookstores and wholesalers at: info@abundantpress.com. Printed in the United States of America- Library of Congress-in-Publication Data. Please note: If you find errors, like spelling or grammar, please send us an email.

Title: NFT Secrets Revealed
Sub-title: The Next Big Asset Breakthrough Everything You Need to Know But were Afraid to Ask
Ver: 12122
Author: Andy Broadaway
1. The main category of the book — Business, Leadership. Marketing, Sales
ISBN: 978-1-948287-34-0

To Get FREE Access Additional Bonuses Visit:

NFTSecretsBook.com

Disclaimer: Although the author(s) and publisher have made every effort to ensure that the information in this book was correct at press time. While we try to keep the information up-to-date and accurate, there are no representations or warranties, express or implied, about the completeness, accuracy, reliability, suitability or availability with respect to the information. The author and publisher are NOT providing tax, legal, financial or investment advice, do not assume and hereby disclaim any liability to any party for any loss, damage, or disruption caused by errors or omissions, whether such errors or omissions result from negligence, accident, or any other cause.

Nothing else contained in this book should be used or construed as an offer to sell, a solicitation of an offer to buy, or a recommendation for any security. Nor is it intended as investment, tax, financial or legal advice. Investors should seek such professional advice for their particular situation.

This book is for informational purposes only. This book should not be considered a solicitation, offer or recommendation for the purchase or sale of any securities or other financial products and services discussed herein. Readers of this book will not be considered clients of Andy Broadaway just by virtue of access to this book. Information contained herein is not intended for persons in any jurisdiction where such distribution or use would be contrary to the laws or regulations of that jurisdiction. Readers should not construe any discussion or information contained herein as personalized advice from Andy Broadaway. Neither our information providers nor we shall be liable for any errors or inaccuracies, regardless of cause, or the lack of timeliness of, or for any delay or loss of income.

Certain information contained in this book is derived from sources that Andy Broadaway and/or believes to be reliable; however, Andy Broadaway and/or does not guarantee the accuracy or timeliness of such information and assumes no liability for any resulting damages. Readers should seek advice regarding the appropriateness of investing in any securities or other financial instruments referred to in this book, website or any other message received from Andy Broadaway and should understand that statements regarding future prospects of these or other financial products may not be realized.

Legal Disclosure: You are hereby advised that Andy Broadaway is not a financial advisor and is NOT providing legal or tax advice. Nothing in this book or its attachments should be interpreted by you as legal advice. For legal advice and all legal related matters, Andy Broadaway recommends that you seek the advice of a qualified attorney licensed in your state or jurisdiction

YOUR RIGHTS: This book is restricted to your personal use only. It does not come with any other rights.

TABLE OF CONTENTS

CHAPTER ONE: WHAT ARE NFTS?	1
CHAPTER: TWO WEB 3.0	19
CHAPTER THREE: WHAT IS A BLOCKCHAIN AND WHY IS IT IMPORTANT?	27
CHAPTER FOUR: THE ONLINE WORLD OF COLLECTIONS	39
CHAPTER 5: THE ART WORLD AND THE NFT	47
CHAPTER 6: THE MARKETPLACE AND NFTS	61
CHAPTER 7: WALLETS, SELLING AND MARKETING	79
CHAPTER 8: MARKETING NFTS	91
CHAPTER 8: QR CODES, AUGMENTED REALITY AND NFTS	95
CHAPTER 9: WHAT IS THE METAVERSE?	105
CASE STUDIES & ARTICLES	111
CONCLUSION	123
GLOSSARY OF TERMS	127

Chapter One
What Are NFTs?

NFTs are the future of ownership. They let us tokenize anything from art, music, and collectibles, all way up to real estate! These tokens only have one official owner at any given time - which means you can't copy/paste a new NFT into existence or modify your record by editing another person's item in this space (unless they give permission).

Instead, everything is secure because it runs on blockchain technology like Ethereum--no one will ever be able change what has already happened here; every transaction legit ends up being recorded permanently on the blockchain.

If you're looking for something exciting and new in the digital currency and asset world? If you're adventurous and always looking to the future and new ways to invest and reap benefits? If these things are true for you, then you need to understand and get into NFTs.

What are NFTs?

They are one of the newest and most exciting forms of digital assets. NFT = Non-Fungible Tokens.

A non-fungible virtual commodity, also can be connected to tangible item with a one of a kind.

Fungible vs. non-fungible

The key difference in fungible versus non-fungible assets can be found in how they're exchanged and traded. While fungible assets can be sold in different forms and exchanges, a non-fungible asset may require a little more time and care to be sold.

Consider the following scenario: you're trying to sell a diamond ring. If it were a fungible good, you could sell the diamond and metal individually — or both together — at an agreed-upon price to various vendors for the same amount of money.

However, the ultimate value of the diamond ring is based on several criteria, including the clarity of the diamond, how the diamond is cut, and what kind of metal the ring is made of. Therefore, the price you would get from a pawn shop may be different than from a jewelry store. Because each diamond ring is unique, it is a non-fungible item.

Examples of fungible assets

We exchange fungible assets on a daily basis without thinking twice. When you buy groceries, get gas for your car, or go on a coffee run, you are exchanging cash for goods and services — or trading fungible items.

Some examples of fungible assets include:

- Currency: Currencies can be exchanged for one another at agreed-upon market rates all across the world and in the digital realm. In whole and fractional numbers, US dollars can be exchanged for Euros, Japanese Yen, or Bitcoin.

- Stocks and mutual funds: When investing in stocks and mutual funds, investors pay cash for a financial instrument that has the same worth as the cash they paid for it at the time of purchase. If a single share of stock costs $5.70, the buyer knows how much they'll have to spend to get several shares, knowing that they can be swapped for cash later.
- Gold and silver are traded at a market rate every day, ensuring that owners know how much worth they have when it's time to buy. When it comes time to sell, someone who has a valuable metal can readily exchange it for cash at market rates, making it fungible.

Examples of non-fungible assets

As mentioned before, while fungible items are interchangeable with each other, non-fungible assets are unique. Therefore, they must be judged across multiple criteria. Some of the factors buyers and sellers consider include provenance (or who owned the item previously), how unique it is compared to others, and how the market for non-fungible assets have changed over time.

In addition, non-fungible assets cannot be broken up and sold in pieces: Its value is determined by the whole of the item.

Some non-fungible assets include:

- **Real estate:** When selling a home, various aspects must be considered, including how much comparable homes have sold for, the demand for properties in the region, and how unique the home is. Real estate is deemed non-fungible since its worth is reliant on certain evaluation factors — such as square footage, architecture, and interior amenities.

- **Trading cards:** Although trading cards are sold in packs of similar value, the actual contents may have varying values depending on their condition, rarity, and composition. Modifiers such as grading and autographs can increase the value. As a result, trade cards are non-fungible due to their unique status.
- Tokens that aren't fungible: Non-fungible assets don't have to be digital tokens. Non-fungible items include family heirlooms, digital treasures, and art collections since they are one-of-a-kind and cannot be directly traded for something of equal worth. Non-fungible tokens have value dependent on the item's rarity and the community that supports it, and no two NFTs are identical.

Non-Fungible Tokens (NFTs) are a type of digital assets, or cryptocurrency. They can represent anything from in game items to securities and other tokens on the blockchain.

NFTs are different than fungible tokens because they hold unique properties that make them less interchangeable with each other like Bitcoin is with every other BTC token.

A non-fungible virtual commodity is a unit of currency on a virtual distributed ledger called a blockchain, in which each NFT represents a unique, digital entity, and so they are essentially not interchangeable. NFTs may represent digital information like art, music, videos, digital items in computer games, and various forms of creative output. A good example of a non-fungal digital product would be a lottery ticket.

They are unique and cannot be copied. They are scarce and they are tradable. If you own an NFT it is unique to you, and it cannot be used by anyone else. Nor can you use anyone else's NFT.

Don't get carried away when you look out at the market and find NFTs skyrocketing in value. Don't jump in feet first until you know what you are looking at and what you are investing in. NFT's are not for everyone but for those who can take advantage of them, they are a steal at the moment. Depending on what line of business you want to invest in, you need to understand a few things about NFTs before you buy.

In today's economy it is even more important than usual to get good value for the money you spend. So, know how your new investments fit into your overall portfolio as you add NFTs to it.

How Do They Work?

For starters, what is Non-Fungible Financial Products? Non-fungal assets are those which are not subject to any kind of market operations that may in any way affect their value. In other words, anything that cannot be destroyed or altered will not be of any use to us and hence is classed as a non-fungible, meaning that no matter how hard we try we cannot make money from it.

How are Non-Fungible tokens created?

NFTs are created by way of tokenization - where tokens (digital items) are issued on the basis of some kind of agreement between two or more entities.

There are many different types of digital assets can be used as NFTs. The most popular include images, video, audio, and music files. Some game developers even allow you to sell your own custom-designed 3D models and characters as NFTs, making them much more valuable than standard ERC-20 tokens.

NFTs are different from ERC-20 tokens, such as DAI or LINK, in that each individual token is completely unique and is not divisible. NFTs give the ability to assign or claim ownership of any unique piece of digital data, trackable by using Ethereum's blockchain as a public ledger.

An NFT is minted from digital objects as a representation of digital or non-digital assets.

For example, an NFT could represent:

- Digital Art:
    - GIF's
    - JPG's
    - Collectibles
    - Music
    - Videos
- Real World Items:
    - Deeds to a car
    - Tickets to a real-world event
    - Tokenized invoices
    - Legal documents
    - Signatures
- Lots and lots more options to get creative with!

An NFT can only have one owner at a time. Ownership is managed through the uniqueID and metadata that no other token can replicate. NFTs are minted through smart contracts that assign ownership and manage the transferability of the NFT's.

When someone creates or mints an NFT, they execute code stored in smart contracts that conform to different standards, such as ERC-721. This information is added to the blockchain where the NFT is being managed.

If you're an artist who wants to sell your work inside a game or app, this is possible using different marketplaces, which I will explain more later in this book. This application works in a very similar way to eBay, but instead of using dollars or other fiat currencies, it uses crypto-tokens and smart contracts, which allow for discussions between buyers and sellers anywhere around the world to take place in near real-time.

Whether the items you buy in games are tradable, vanity items, or trade goods, they all work in pretty much the same way. If you've ever bought something in an online store with Steam or downloaded a mobile application that added it to your account for later use, then you already know the basic process involved in buying NFT's.

First, the website or application you're buying from creates a new record in its database about the item you're purchasing.

The game's server does this automatically whenever it receives information about your purchase. This record will contain all of the information about the item except ownership. It will show who made and sold it, how much they sold it for, and where that sale took place (which may be on a different server). It will also include a list of the recent transactions in the item so that you could check to see whether it was resolved or canceled if there was a dispute.

Once this record is made, it's communicated to all of the nodes on the network so that they can verify that it's valid. Next, your record is updated as well. This will contain information about who actually holds ownership of this item and how much they spent, along with other details such as: where you are located (your country), what time your purchase was made and how long you've had an account with this website or application.

Once the item is on your account, you can either use it as currency for purchasing items in-game or a vanity token. Alternatively, you can hold onto it to see if its value appreciates.

NFT's and Games

NFTs used to be mostly associated with video games as they allowed game developers to create items with rare attributes or spawn in different levels or regions of the game world with widely varying values depending on what they offer and where they spawn in the virtual world. But NFT's can easily be used in all types of different blockchain applications since they are an excellent way for developers to monetize their games and provide players with a fun and engaging ways to interact with the game.

When playing a game or interacting with a blockchain-based application that uses NFT's, you will often find yourself coming across a scarce item. These items could be unique clothing or weapons that could give your character an advantage in the game or an opportunity to win some valuable in-game prizes and rewards.

However, the rarity of these items means that they are usually priced far above what most players are willing to pay. This means that it's almost impossible for the average player to get their hands on them. Almost but not quite. In this book I will tell you how you can buy or win NFTs that are rare but not so expensive yet.

We will also look at how you can use these NFT's to make an extra income out of your hobby or get a quick profit from some of the items you find valuable.

Since NFT's are very rare, unique, and tradable, they can be used as a means of currency when playing games online. They also make it easy to create an in-game economy and give players a way to earn money through trading or selling NFT's to other players. Most digital currencies don't offer much value outside of the blockchain applications from which they originate.

However, this is not the case with NFT's and other digital assets tied to an application. When you acquire these assets, you automatically become a part of the blockchain and gain access to the in-game economy and other services within the application, which will allow you to use your assets anywhere in the world.

For this reason alone, NFT's have become extremely popular with many blockchain-based applications and online games. Whenever a new game comes out that uses NFT's, it can become a valuable asset in itself and continue to gain value as more people get involved in the game. These new users will also create more NFT's, and the game economy will continue to grow and expand.

In many cases, NFT's have taken the place of traditional digital currencies because they offer players many of the same benefits without having to worry about their value dropping on an open market or them being stolen from you. I will discuss in a later chapter specifically how players can use NFTs.

How can an asset become an NFT? Or Non-Fungible?

NFTs are digital images, videos and audio that can be uniquely identified by the blockchain. Unlike cryptocurrency dollar bills or stocks which are all collectively limited in supply to 21 million copies each--NFTs provide a unique asset for ownership with no such limitations! You're getting something special when you purchase an NAF token because not only will your investment have real world value as part of this new economy; but also, there's

100% chance it won't ever be replicated again due its uniqueness on top of being non-fundable unlike most other assets.

What good is a million-dollar house if you can't prove that it's yours? Digital files on the blockchain are no different; they're unique and there will never be another exactly like them. If someone else claims to have something similar, then we'll know for sure what our true assets really worth when faced with an attempt at infringement!

By guaranteeing the uniqueness of its digital file, it can increase in value. The proof that this is a unique product and you cannot destroy or alter any copy at all because they're on every computer connected to blockchain technology! For example, your transaction is written to the blockchain for everyone to see this is called a smart contract.

And NFT on the blockchain has a digital certificate of authenticity. And all you need to do is look at what's called an "artwork" for verification!

A Digital Certificate of Authenticity (DCOA) has your name on it and can't be deleted or altered in any way because they're sealed with encryption technology, so nobody but YOU have the ownership.

How are they changing the marketplace?

In the past, artists had to rely on traditional methods like selling their work at galleries or giving presentations during art shows. But thanks largely due NFTs-a new form of digital collectibles that allow users from all around world buy and sell original artwork using cryptocurrency-, these days any artist can be successful without leaving home!

Take 12-year-old who helped create an innovative collection used by many merchants today including Nike (and formerly Starbucks) amongst others - her idea has already made $5 million dollars within three weeks' time; not bad considering she's only twelve years.

One person paid 1.3 million for a picture of rock! I had to look it up and that's not even half the price, but this piece was sold at Sotheby's auction house in New York City where they brought in 26 million with their board-aoke NFT bundle deal-- so over $26 Million on top of what you would expect from an original work? Well sure enough -the JPEG artwork has broken records as well; coming close (if not exceeding) prices seen during last year's peak crypto craze when one pixel sold online for nearly 70,000 dollars.

The way we live and work is changing rapidly. Technology has transformed our lives in ways that were unimaginable just a few years ago, with the digital age being one of them! Generation Z (or "GenZ") grew up immersed into these currents - they've never known anything else than constant connectivity. This means many things for businesses like yours: an ever-growing customer base who are used to getting everything on demand; younger workers know how quickly information spreads online so security precautions need be extra careful...

There is the biggest wealth transfer in human history happening over the next 25 years, $68 trillion is going to go from one generation to this digital generation over the next 25 years. And this has even been talked about CNBC right here. Know what does this mean for financial advisors?

The massive wealth transfer to a digital generation is only the beginning. The next major issue lurking in this transition are severe shortages of assets, which will have lasting effects on our society as well!

What's The Difference Between Tokens, Coins, and NFTs?

With all the information on the market about tokens and cryptocurrencies, why a whole book on NRFs? What makes NTFs so different from the other forms of coins and from tokens? Let's review for those of you who are new to this market. Again, if you are an expert in this than just jump ahead to Chapter four.

There are significant differences between the tokens and coins we are familiar with and an NFT. The three ways to use digital assets are crypto-tokens, ERC-20 tokens or coins, and NFTs. If you are reading this book, you probably have at least some rudimentary knowledge of tokens and coins.

The ERC-20 tokens are made to create new transactions or crypto-assets. They have no monetary value outside the very specific exchanges they are sold on. Crypto-tokens are the most popular with the blockchains and most use ERC-20 tokens in their development. Obviously the most complex of these types is the NFT, because they represent those unique assets inside an application as discussed earlier. Also, you can use the very same ERC-20 technology that is used for most other crypto currencies.

The NFT's are not only fun to use, but as we have seen they also provide so many benefits such as: removing ambiguity, increasing the transparency of a business process, allowing you to remain anonymous, improving the security of your assets, and much more! They can be used on various platforms, which means that it will be possible for you to make a profit by collecting them. NFTs are dynamic and profitable. They can be used in many different ways, for many different reasons. NFTs can help you to efficiently start an online business and the blockchain will give you all the tools you'll need to be profitable.

Gaming

This is why gamers are so excited about NFTs assets in their games. There are currently many different ways in which you can use NFT's in a game. Many games have them as tradable assets that you can buy from other players and sell to others when you're finished using them or even trade with other players for items or services within the game. Other games allow you to use NFT's as currency for paying the costs associated with playing the game itself, such as items like better weapons, armour, or other equipment.

If you are using NFT's in a game to pay for in-game items, then it is likely that their value will diminish over time. However, since the assets are tied to your account and yours alone, it is more difficult for someone else to take them off you. Also, the same applies when you want to use them as currency inside the game. Whenever there is an increase in demand for NFT's in a game or application, they tend to go up in value so long as their use inside the game continues.

In some online games that let you create your own character and design something unique for yourself or your friends, NFT's can be used as vanity tokens. You can buy NFT's that already look like your character and use them as a shortcut to the process of creating one. In games that have NFT's as collectibles, you may be able to add them to your collection by finding them out in the open world or earning them through gameplay. These types of NFT's are typically not tradeable or sellable, so it is impossible for anyone but you (or an administrator) to take them away from you.

Which Tokens Will Be Most Popular?

Not all tokens are created equal. Some are much more popular than others and have more value because they're tied directly into games or applications where their use could cause an increase in demand. This makes them easier to trade than other types of crypto assets like ERC-20 tokens and NFTs.

We have found that the most popular tokens are those that came from games and apps. They tend to significantly impact the price of other crypto-assets because they can have a more substantial impact on their overall demand compared to standard ERC-20 tokens. These include different game currencies such as those used by video games and mobile apps.

Here is a look at the top 10 NFT projects by sales volume (as of 11-21-2020)

- Axie Infinity: $169.4 million, -20.2%
- Bored Ape Yacht Club: $88.0 million, +46.0%
- Mutant Ape Yacht Club: $59.2 million, +54.5%
- The Sandbox: $45.6 million, +200.3%
- Wolf Game: $36.8 million, N/A
- Farmers World: $35.2 million, +18.9%
- CryptoPunks: $33.5 million, -31.0%
- Doodles: $28.8 million, +348.7%
- Art Blocks: $18.0 million, -41.1%
- Cool Cats: $9.7 million, +37.4%
- Reported by CryptoSlam. November 21, 2021

How Are Initial Coin Offerings Conducted?

ICOs are relatively easy to conduct. All you need to do is create a smart contract. This needs to represent a specific number of tokens that have been created for the purposes of the ICO. For example, suppose your application is being created as a decentralized journalism platform. In that case, you can set aside tokens or cryptocurrencies that have been designed to be used specifically for the purchase of news and services within that application.

These tokens will be tied into an ICO process. They will usually be sold during a crowd sale or fundraising event in return for legal tender or other cryptocurrencies to raise money for development costs.

Other Uses

Today one of the main uses of NTFs is in the digital art world. You can purchase an NTF of an original piece of digital art. You then own that original just like you would a work of art that is on a physical canvas.

NFT's can also be associated with digital data that is easily reproduced. This would include, videos, audio files and photos. They can be associated at the same time with unique digital files that are verified authentic by blockchain technology. You can own the original file, yet copies can still be made and shared. However, the NFT's are not interchangeable, and this is what sets them apart from Bitcoin and other cryptocurrencies.

The NFT is a new type of asset. It might be the most important advancement in finance history. If you sleep on this, it's going to be like sleeping on the internet or domains, being a valuable property. We're going to talk about examples or sleeping on mobile. When that came out, gaming and apps, this is that level of sophistication.

As you know an asset is simply anything that has value and can be transferred. It can be a watch or a Bitcoin. It might be a domain name or intellectual property. To be an NFT it must have value and it must be transferrable. It also must be provable that you purchased that asset. Buy a Bitcoin and millions of computers will record the purchase on the Ethereum network.

NFTs can be so much more than we see now. This could include:

- Redemption codes, gifts or coupons
- Tickets for concerts, cinemas, and other events
- To underline the authenticity of products, including art and fashion.
- And of course, for digital collectibles and in-game assets.

The NFT was first launched on the Ethereum blockchain in 2015. The value of NFT's grew along with other cryptocurrencies. In 2021 NFT sales were over $2 billion in the first quarter. It ended the 2021 year at $41 billion worth of Ethereum-based NFTs were sold, (according to Chainalysis research cited by the Financial Times.)

Compared this to the global art market was worth ~$50 billion

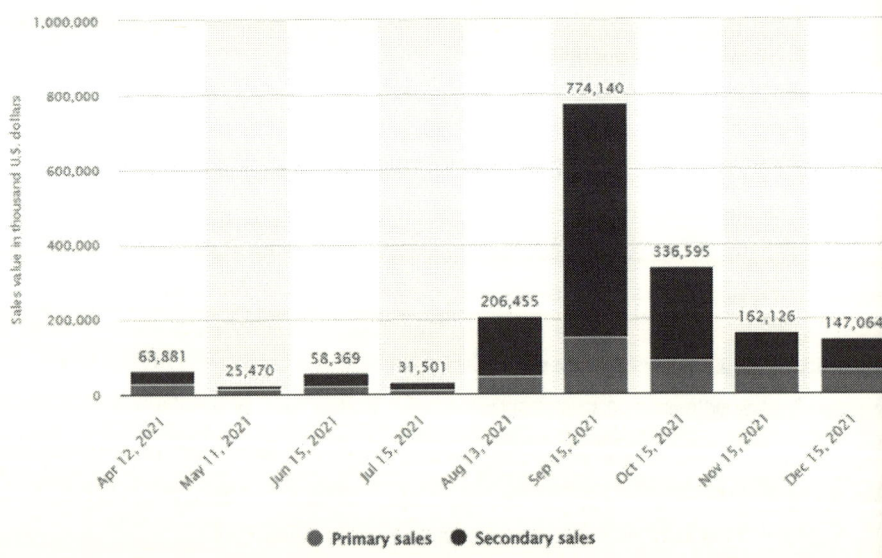

Source: https://www.statista.com/

The vast majority (75%) of NFT transactions were sales under $10,000, but the wealthiest 9% of NFT wallets held ~80% of the market's value.

Non-fungible tokens (NFTs) are a type of digital asset that exists as an individual item. While they might seem confusing to many people, one thing is clear – NFT token popularity continues its steady rise over time with more interesting developments happening this year than ever before! For example: In 2021 alone there have been several notable statistics surrounding these new technologies...

2021 Summary

1. Most Expensive NFT Sold for Nearly $92 Million.
2. Beeple's First Physical Work Sold for Nearly $30 Million.
3. NFT Trading Volume Added Up to Nearly $11 Billion in Q3.
4. People from China and Singapore Are the Most Interested in NFTs.
5. The Most Expensive NFT Video Sold for Almost $7 million.
6. The Most Expensive NFT Meme Sold for $4 Million.
7. The Majority of NFTs Sell for Less Than $200.
8. Each Day 1000s of NFT Sales Are Made.
9. NFT Sales Amount to Millions Per Week.
10. There Were Close to 40,000 Unique Buyers in March 2021.
11. The NFT Market Grew Almost Tenfold in Two Years.
12. NFT Sales Amounted to Over $2.4 Billion in the First 6 Months of 2021.
13. OpenSea's Trading Volume Increased by 800+%.
14. Twitter Founder Sells the First Tweet via an NFT Marketplace.
15. NBA's Top Shots Has Already Made $700+ Million.
16. NFTs for Gaming Declined.
17. Kings of Leon Released an Album as an NFT.

18. Taco Bell Released 25 NFTs.
19. More Than a Third of E-sports Fans are Interested in NFTs.
20. Men Are the Most Likely to Collect NFTs.

Is this because they are different and more valuable than other digital assets? They are scarce and they are tradable. Is factors make them unique. They cannot be sold to a second person nor traded on an open market once you have purchased them. Because it is created on a blockchain you can never reproduce or copy it. Every NFT is unique and there is only one of each NFT. These factors have made the NFT highly valuable and very expensive.

If you are scratching your head about now wondering what in the world is a blockchain, the next chapter is for you.

Conclusion

The NFT's are a revolutionary way to do business, and they're going change the world. Not only will it be possible for you remove any ambiguity in your process or make yourself more anonymous while doing so; these tokens also give people an opportunity to turn their assets into cash!

You could collect them on various platforms which means that even if one falls apart (which doesn't seem likely), there'll still plenty left over from what was collected before--so no worries here either customers/investors alike should invest wisely because this new technology has got lots of potential where many other methods don't offer anything close.

Chapter Two
Web 3.0

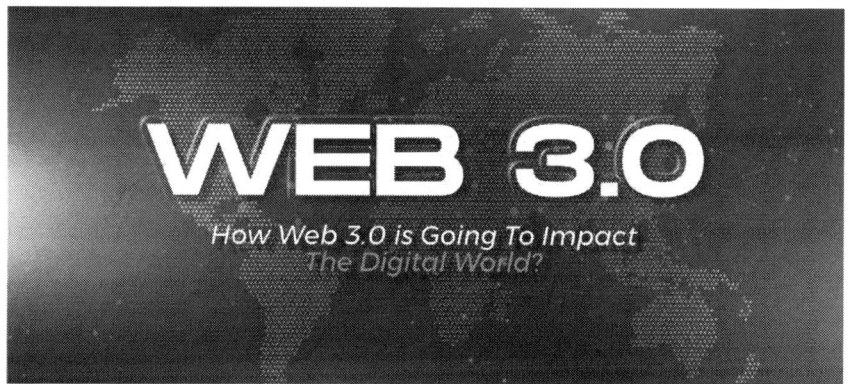

As I said in chapter one, if you know all there is to know about blockchains, then skip this chapter. If not, in order to understand the NFT and their value, you must understand Web 3.0 or blockchains. What is Web 3.0 and what does it have to do with blockchains? In order to understand NFTs, you need to understand Web 3.0 and blockchains.

There have already been two different incarnations of the WWW. This 3.0 version is a major change from how the web has allowed sites to be designed and how users can interact with those websites.

This means that websites will be easier to use and there will be more smart and intuitive applications. A good example of a smarter application is a smarter search engine that takes the user right to what he wants without having to sort through an abundance of choices.

The key here is the use of something like artificial intelligence to understand what the searcher wants instead of matching keywords.

Let's look back a second

Web 1.0 is the predecessor to modern day internet, where it was primarily read-only and had hyperlinks connecting pages together instead of videos or other interactive media content with end users who could do nothing on their own device besides navigate between these websites without any interactivity whatsoever!

Web 2.0 is the internet today, and it's miles ahead of Web 1.0 in terms of how often you can interact with content on your screen! Back when I was first starting out as a blogger myself (way back when 2000!), there were only two publishing platforms that everyone used- WordPress or Blogger.

But nowadays we have so many more options like Tumblr & Facebook & Instagram are where people share pictures instantaneously and instantly. Where us as users are encouraged to post and contribute their own content in order for more interactive than ever before!

This is a total recreation of the web, as opposed to the evolutions displayed in Web 2.0.

When will 3.0 be available and what will it look like? We don't know 100% yet as the technology for it is not yet matured.

Web 3.0 is coming and it's going to change how we interact with the internet forever! Some say that this next evolutionary stage of web technology will be more functional than previous ones while others predict an ideology shift as well, but one thing remains certain: Kids these days are going through significant changes in their daily lives because they're growing up surrounded by digitalization every day--whether you like it or not.

The coming generation of the internet will fundamentally be:

Open or transparent

More open network than previous generations of the internet because it's built on top of an open-source software protocol that ensures transparency and accessibility for all developers around world. The new Web unprecedentedly combines both private blockchains with public ones, providing increased safety while still remaining decentralized across networks

Trustless

The blockchain is a trustless network that ensures no intermediaries interfere in any online transactions or interactions. One example of truthfulness would be the popular use for cryptocurrencies, which are mostly conducted through this technology's capabilities

Decentralized

Data being stored at multiple secure locations on the internet. This will eliminate any **data-loss threats** *and break the massive data silos that hold our data.*

Here's a model of what it may look like.

Today in 2.0 you can use the search function to find keywords and the most popular information. The most popular information, not necessarily the most accurate or interesting information. Even as we are all adding "quality content" to our websites, 2.0 cannot really understand it.

Web 3.0 will understand the context through its artificial intelligent assistant. This AI will know the user, understands the user and personalizes the information it gives to the user.

Web 1.0 was in place through 2000 or so. Information was on servers and users could interact with the server in a less than sophisticated way. Search engines, Amazon, Ebay and others were just beginning.

Web 2.0 came into use shortly after 2000 with more collaborative and interactive abilities. Bandwidth improvements greatly contributed to this evolution of the web. With 2.0 came smartphones, games and apps and almost real time activities. Now here comes Myspace, Facebook, Twitter, and Instagram. There were new multiplayer games with great graphics and a whole world of esports came alive. Machine learning algorithms and Big Data joined the party. _Inter Planetary File System_

Artificial Intelligence or AI defines Web 3.0. This leads to intelligent interactions between software and software. This is a breakthrough. It is actually blockchain technology that allows 3.0 to create IPFS or peer to peer file systems. IPFS leaps over what HTTP can do. It is so much more secure that the SSL is not needed. All versions of a file are kept. Data does not necessarily live on just one certain server. It can be distributed across the system.

In IPFS the address is related to the content not key words. So, if the content moves you do not have to update the address. It is more like the systems that have multiple servers the hold data and also request it. It will work with any transport layer such as Bluetooth.

Growing out of the blockchain, 3.0 will have the ability to create and hold digital identities. This is a critical development than could stop a lot of cyber-crime in its tracks.

Unlike 2.0 interactions in 3.0 between computers will be verifiable. Each user can have one specific digital ID that no one else has, linked to a document that verifies identity. This will virtually eliminate cybercrime and allow individual users to manage their own personal data.

This new paradigm changes how websites are developed but even more it changes how users will interact with websites. Life will be easier and searches will be more accurate with 3.0. For PC users life is becoming more intuitive all the time.

Applications are smarter and understand your needs better. You will think you are in the world of artificial intelligence when you use the smart search functions on 3.0. Web 3.0 is being launched by one company in late November of 2021 and the launch should be complete by early January 2022. This Web 3.0 will be decentralized, secure and verifiable.

In the world of technologies, it is a broad-based movement bringing 3.0 software to all of us without needing intermediaries like Facebook, Google and others. There is no central authority that controls 3.0. As you continue through this book, keep this in mind. This decentralized lack of authoritative control is a major aspect of the success of NFTs.

Bitcom and the Ethereum blockchain are very involved with 3.0 and goals are in line with the goals of 3.0. Most cryptocurrencies are open source, secure, and decentralized blockchains.

To exemplify this, Gavin Wood, the co-founder of Ethereum, has written of 3.0 that it is *"the foundation of the freedom of the individual against the arbitrary authority of the despot. Platform monopolies like Google and Facebook are the despots."* *"If society does not adopt the principles of Web 3.0 for its digital platform,"* Wood continued, *"it runs the risk of continued corruption and* eventual failure, just as medieval feudal systems and Soviet-style communism proved untenable in a world of modern democracies." For these developers Web 3.0 offers a potential utopia of freedom in cyberspace.

At the Web 3.0 Summit of 2018, the founder and CEO of Protocol Labs blockchain based industry stated that with 3.0 *"The internet is becoming its own nation."* With the dawn of smart contracts that cannot be modified once put in place, everything business knows about cyberspace and our way of life could change.

Cryptocurrencies and NFTs will be at the heart of this change. As the Securities and Exchanges Commission said in a statement the *"Digital landscape is evolving and decentralized finance is challenging financial products, intermediation, and financial markets."*

I said I was going to discuss the blockchain and I have spent a lot of time on Web 3.0 even though it is not in operation yet. This is because the blockchain is a fundamental aspect of 3.0. Just as we would not have NFTs without blockchains, we won't have 3.0 without them either. Both the digital IDs and the distributed files are re blockchains.

Most important of all the blockchain creates cryptocurrencies and allows them to be used to make payments – micropayments that is. The cryptocurrency allows for payments no matter how small. This means you can sell things for a few pennies a piece.

This was not possible before blockchains and cryptocurrencies. Without them NFT's would not be possible either. However, by 2025, with Web 3.0 and blockchains everywhere, applications that use computer resources with produce and use 160 times the amount of data we were using in 2010. We are almost there now.

Web 3.0 is the following stage in the development of the web, the foundations of which have effectively been laid. Speculated to be a hyper-savvy network fit for understanding data like a human, web 3.0 will be a monstrous jump in network innovation according to current principles.

Aside from the innovative wonders that web 3.0 guarantees, it additionally proposes the execution of specific philosophies that will radically modify the current business as usual of the present organizations. Furthermore, we as the end web 2.0 it will usher into Web 3.0, the obscure the lines between the genuine and the virtual will be blurred.

Chapter Three
What is a Blockchain and Why is it Important?

Basically, a blockchain is a record of all transactions associated with an item usually sold online. A blockchain is a record that can be seen, and can be verified by anyone choosing to do so. When an item such as Bitcoin is purchased, received or given, there is a record of that transaction.

Cryptocurrencies would not be possible without blockchain technology. It is the blockchain that allows you to transfer value (cryptocurrencies) online without a credit card company or a bank. You can't do that with any other currency or value that can be transferred.

Just imagine how much easier your finances would be if you could access anything – international and national – with just your smart phone or tablet. If you have an internet connection, you have access with blockchains. The blockchain verifies the transaction and makes it both secure and accurate. The record of transactions is contained by several linked computers in a peer-to-peer network. It sounds complicated but you don't have to know how a blockchain is created to be able to use it effectively.

In fact, you probably use blockchains now without knowing it.

If you want to know the transactional history of an item such as a Bitcoin, just look at the blockchain for evidence of what has happened. All the major cryptocurrencies are secured in this manner. This includes Bitcoin, Bitcoin Cash, Ethereum, Litecoin and many NFTs.

The verification that blockchains can produce allow individuals who never met to exchange secure payments without having to go through a bank, a credit card company or a site like PayPal.

Payments made between individuals using blockchain technology is more secure than your debit or credit card transactions.

NFTs are more secure than that payment you just made on PayPal or Google pay. Although many people think only of cryptocurrencies when they think of blockchains, but the technology is so much more.

Blockchains are use for so much more than cryptocurrencies just as NFTs are used for so much more than gaming. Blockchains are being developed that improve healthcare records and explore medical research. Other stream various supply chains. Just like NFTs are found more in the online art world than perhaps in gaming these days.

Benefits of Blockchains

There are many benefits to the blockchain, especially in respect to cryptocurrencies. Here are just a few.

- Blockchains are an open-source software. What does this mean? It means if you understand code the software to develop blockchains is open source to anyone to review. The license for open-source software grants all users the right to change, use, or distribute the software and code freely. You can share it with anyone for any reason. It is this aspect of the blockchain software that makes every transaction on a cryptocurrency network is transparent, verified and recorded. Anyone can access this verification. Because of this there is no manipulation, no theft, and no worry about identity theft.
- Blockchains are international and anything developed in a blockchain can be sent anywhere at any time with less expense and less time used. Both cryptocurrencies and NFTs can be sent around the world quickly and inexpensively.
- Payments using blockchains are a lot more private than using a credit card or a debit to make an online purchase. No personal information is needed with a blockchain product. You don't have to give your name, address and email address. So, you won't get as much junk mail either.
- Blockchains eliminate the middleman – PayPal, banks and credit card companies. This preserves your privacy with personal information, and it makes it possible for you to save money and time.

Remember crypto currencies are NOT blockchain. Crypto currencies are digital money as the technology that makes them possible is the blockchain. There are thousands of different blockchains with many different functions. From here on I will be concerned with teaching you about NFTs and the blockchains they are developed with.

Review NFTs

Knowing what blockchains are now and how NFTs fit into that picture, let's review just a little about the NFT itself. How is the NFT different from other digital assets? The most important aspect is they are scarce. Once an NFT is created on the blockchain, it can never be copied or reproduced. This means that there will only ever be one version of each NFT. We have said that they are also tradable by the person who owns them.

But, unlike many digital assets, this can't be sold to other players or traded with others on an open market.

Anyone who wants to can market NFTs online. You can easily create them and sell them. As an investor you can buy and sell them online. It's a fairly simply process of buying them and storing them in an NFT wallet. I will cover this in detail in a later chapter.

How much profit you can make depends as usual on the current market and how well you market your NFTs. You can also buy NFTs using specifically an Ethereum wallet and sell them later.

If you're thinking about using non-fungible tokens for selling your digital assets, then it's essential to realize that there are many different reasons why you should buy these tokens in the first place. This includes the fact that they're more secure than other types of digital coins because they have been designed in a specific way.

This also means that there are fewer ways to lose money if you own them because there's no other way to lose this asset accidentally. All that you need to do is make sure that the market value of these tokens increases over time so you can use them for a profit at any time.

The specific blockchain that NFTs are a part of is the Ethereum blockchain. Even more so NTFs are Ethereum-specific. What this means is that NFTs cannot be created except with the tools inherent in the Ethereum blockchain.

In the gaming world this meant that you had to own a game that had NFTs in it and have a copy of those NFTs to use. Once you had those things in your game, you could make money from the NFT. This is especially true if you're lucky enough to come across one in-game and not have to pay the higher asking price for it.

This makes NFT's much more complex than many other types of digital assets because you first need to own a game with NFT's, and then you need to have a copy of the same NFT in that game in order to use it. But once you have both these things, it becomes relatively easy for you to make money from them.

This same type of process has carried over to many other aspects of life than just gaming. The online art world is one of the examples I will explain in more detail. The online world of collecting art and other items is a NFTs driven world. NFTs are driven by the Ethereum. Let's take a closer look at the Ethereum.

Ethereum

(Warning: this section is very details and might be boring)

Just what is the Ethereum? Yes, it is a blockchain, so what makes it different and what makes it best for developing NFTs? It is an open source, decentralized blockchain and it has smart contract functions. I will discuss smart contracts in detail in a later chapter. The cryptocurrency native to this blockchain is Ether or ETH. This cryptocurrency is the second largest market capitalization with only Bitcoin being larger.

It was in 2013 that Vitalik Buterin first had the idea for Ethereum. Using crowdfunding to pay for the development, the platform was live by July of 2015. What made Ethereum different? It allowed anyone with minimum knowledge to place decentralized applications on the platform that all users can interact with. That is the essence of open sourcing. However open sourced, decentralized financial applications were new and exciting. No brokers, no banks, exchanges or middle men were needed for the ordinary person to engage on Ethereum.

One could borrow or lend against their cryptocurrency assets. It is on this platform that anyone can create and exchange NFTs as well as many other cryptocurrencies operating as ERC-20 tokens o the Ethereum blockchain.

As soon as Ethereum was up and running developers were already upgrading the platform. Buterin believed that platforms for Bitcoin and other blockchains could be used for more than just financial currency transactions. With NFTs you can do more than just trade currency as we will see in the next chapter. In order to accomplish this, Ethereum needed a language with which to develop applications that could attach stocks and real estate as well as digital assets to the blockchain.

Earlier in 2013, Buterin thought to do this with an existing blockchain and partnered with eToro to accomplish this. This project however failed because the two CEOs could not agree on the process for moving forward. He then went about developing a brand-new platform with the kind of programming language called a Turing complete programming language. This became Ethereum.

All the developers of Ethereum met during the North American Bitcoin Conference in 2014. Here they worked to finalize the project. Later on, it was decided to launch the product as a non-Profit enterprise.

Even though the group that met at the conference were primary developers, there are more than 8 actual developers.

Development

The Ethereum was developed in Switzerland with a critical aspect being embedding an executable smart contract in the blockchain itself. Gavin Wood was the chief technology officer and did this work. Funded by a crowd sale where participants used Bitcoin to purchase ETH. 2018 the Ethereum blockchain was the 2nd largest. Buterin named the blockchain from a list of elements.

Prior to launching the actual product several prototypes were tried. For the last prototype/beta users/testers received 25,000 ETH. The official launch came in July 2015. There have been several planned updates since 2015 including incentive structures and increased functionality. There have been 4 network upgrades since then.

Another crowd sale for the decentralized autonomous organization was held in 2016 to the tune of 150 million USD. Then a hacker stole 50 million USD equivalent DAO tokens. In response the platform was split into Ethereum and Ethereum Classic. The Ethereum platform continued to deal with attacks in 2016.

Then in 2017 a group of 30 founding members formed the Enterprise Ethereum Alliance (EEA), spearheaded by several Fortune 500 companies and several startup blockchains. Within months the nonprofit has 116 and in less than 6 months they had over 150. Soon many major corporations were bringing their cryptocurrencies to the Ethereum blockchain. This included a consortium of MasterCard, JP Morgan Chase and USB investing 65 million USD into a software company using the Ethereum infrastructure.

Soon there will be a major 2.0 upgrade to Ethereum or ETH2. This upgrade will increase the speed of transactions from 15 per second to tens of thousands per second. This will increase the NFT transactions tremendously. The final phase of 2.0 is scheduled to drop in 2022.

How it Works

So how does a blockchain like Ethereum really work? It is a network of computers in a non-hierarchical, permissionless system. These computers or nodes build a consensus on batches of transactions or blocks that form the blockchain. Whenever a block is added a transaction is also executed. This changes the values and balances in the accounts which are stored separately from the blockchain. Each one of the nodes communicates only with a small group of other nodes called peers. When a new transaction comes onto the blockchain, the node sends it to its peers and they send it to their peers. The chain is built in this way throughout the network.

Then specialized nodes, -miners- keep track of all these transactions and use them to build new blocks in the chain. These new blocks are sent to the rest of the network. All new blocks are checked for security and validity. Because of the open source, non-hierarchical nature of the network, there can be competing chains. When this happens, the network decides which chain is the primary or canonical chain. The losing chain is abandoned by the network.

It sounds funny but in this virtual world the cryptocurrency, ETH is generated as a reward for the work the miners do in adding blocks to the chain. ETH is the only currency that the Ethereum blockchain will accept.

So how does the ETH compare with the more well-known Bitcoin? Bitcoin is a digital currency while Ether can be a digital currency, but Ethereum can also create NFTs, smart contracts and run decentralized applications. With Bitcoin the network validates every ten minutes while Ethereum validates every twelve seconds! Ethereum has no cap to their supply while Bitcoin is limited to 21,000,000 coins.

Ethereum is also more application savvy than Bitcoin. In addition to NFTs and FTs, Ethereum can work with DAOs (decentralized autonomous organizations), crowdfunding, games, initial coin offerings, decentralized exchanges and finances, gambling and prediction markets.

Let's take a quick look at some of these applications.

Decentralization

There are many aspects of decentralization in the Ethereum blockchain. An important factor to consider is that many of these DApps are able to be integrated into package of decentralized financial applications. These applications included DeFi or Decentralized finance, a dinancial instrument that was outside the control of the usual mainstream of companies and government regulations.

This instrument gave ordinary people the ability to invest and earn interest in a simple and safe way. Applications such as MetaMask, Maker DAO and Unswap were all geared to a decentralized financial world built for the middle-class investor in tokens.

In 2020 alone, this market grew from 20 million to 2.9 billion.

NFT's on the Flow blockchain.

NFT's have been a part of the world for around a decade now. However, it was the introduction of the Ethereum blockchain that made them famous again. Soon after this, they were introduced to other platforms as well. The Flow blockchain is one such platform that offers NFT's that are ideal for business users. It provides an easy way to add assets into the world of tokens and cryptocurrency and provides companies with an alternative set of tools in which they can use to ensure that they have a smooth business process on their hands.

Since it works on the Ethereum network, you can expect that you will get all of the benefits of using a platform like this one. This means that it will be easier for you to make purchases using these tokens in a secure and hassle-free manner. The Flow blockchain is a one of a kind blockchain, providing for the customization of cryptocurrencies in anyway the user wants.

You or your business controls how what you develop will look. Here is where you get your rare or unique NFTs. They can't be duplicated and if you own them, you can make a profit from them. There is a link to the Flow blockchain website in the references at the end of this book.

The Ether has become the second largest cryptocurrency behind only Bitcoin. However, Ethers have continued to boom even as Bitcoin sales have slowed. This has everything to do with the dramatic growth of NFTs in the online art world.

The next chapter is dedicated to an in-depth look at this digital art world and how NFTs work within it to create, sell, trade and buy digital images. 2021 has seen a tremendous growth in new Ethereum accounts. In the first quarter of 2021 Ethereum transactions were reported to be 1.5 trillion USD. At the same time a 2021 bond issue in ETH by the European Investment Bank was worth 120 million USD. The investment community as well as the creative community are3 taking notice of the capabilities of the Ethereum blockchain NFTs.

NFTs and decentralized financials have brought a real world profit to the Ethereum blockchain leading to even more investments. Defi protocols have resulted in an increase from 900 million USD to 68 billion USD from 2020 to 2021.

How are non-fungible crypto assets used?

Non-fungible crypto-assets can represent almost anything that you'd like them to mean. This could include different types of virtual goods or items, artwork, or even physical assets like real estate. It's possible to use them to represent any type of object that can be unique somehow. You can also sell them on an NFT Marketplace so that people can buy and sell them in exchange for other forms of cryptocurrencies such as bitcoin and Ethereum.

The critical thing to understand is that these assets cannot be duplicated or hacked in any way due to the fact they are digital tokens that are tied explicitly into their own smart contract.

They're also very secure because they are created using smart contracts which have been programmed by the ERC-721 token standard, which means that hackers or criminals cannot exploit them in any way.

Chapter Four
The Online World of Collections

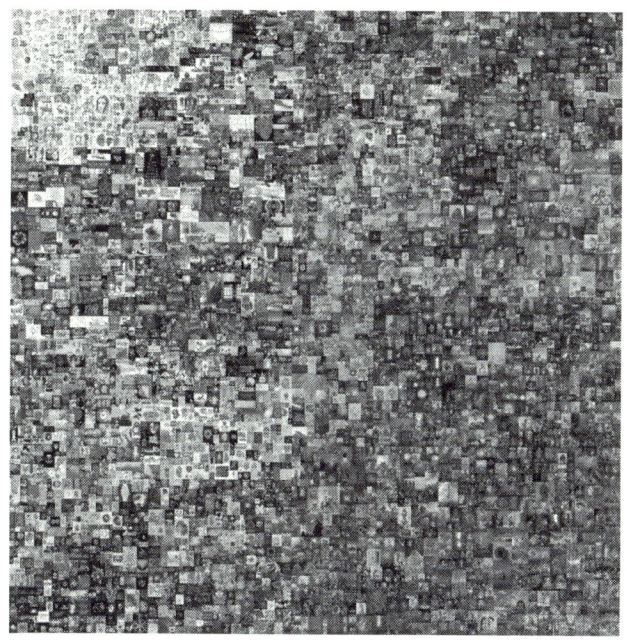

Beeple's Everydays: The First 5000 Days (2021) sold for $69 million in March.

COURTESY CHRISTIE'S IMAGES LTD. 2021

Why Do People Collect?

Perhaps before we look at the role of NFTs with online collections – especially art collections – we should look at why people collect at all. The current explosion in the use of NFTs is in the online art world with all the hype and the growing ability to execute the sales.

Since the $69 million sale of Beeple's Everydays: The First 5000 Days (seen above) at Christie's on March 11, a set of devoted collectors of non-fungible tokens, or NFTs, has started to emerge.

The mystery buyer of that record-setting digital artwork, the online sale of which made Beeple the third-highest-selling living artist, behind David Hockney and Jeff Koons, was soon after revealed to be Singapore-based crypto investor Vignesh Sundaresan, aka MetaKovan.

Using his virtual pseudonym, the 32-year-old entrepreneur and founder of the Metapurse NFT project beat out Chinese tech billionaire Justin Sun, who took to Twitter to announce he'd lost the bid for Everydays by a razor-thin margin.

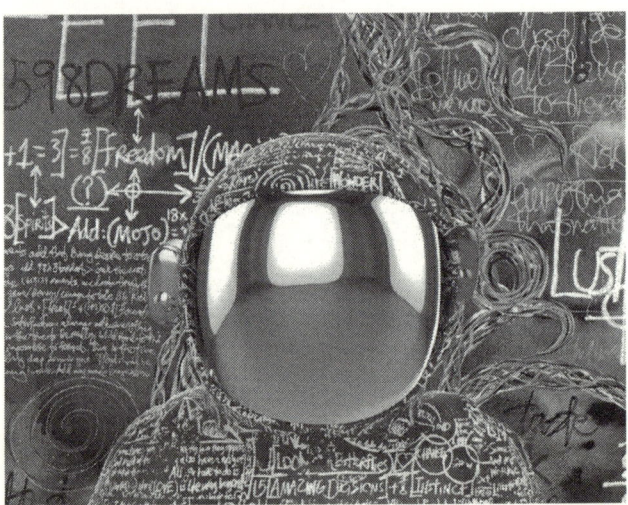

Another example is Brendan Murphy's Boonji Project. (above) This project shows us what is possible when a project challenges the realm of possibility in generative art, utility, and community.

Boonji Project launched on October 21, 2021, and through its Dutch auction, sold out in one of the biggest primary on-sales of all time at an average price of .42 ETH ($1727 USD).

In less than 4 hours, the project has already seen over 1,000 ETH in transaction volume.

In advance of the highly anticipated launch, Boonji Project amassed an eruptive cult following on Discord with over 134,000 members.

Before I get into the art world too heavily let's look at the motivation of folks who are doing the collecting.

Most people collect something even if they don't think of themselves as a collector. There's an enormous variety in the kinds of things that people like to collect. It might be pictures, books, vinyl records, toys, dinnerware and much, much more.

So why do we want to gather up these things?

Well, there are several reasons for this collecting as well.

There are two types of collectors. Those who do it professionally and those who do it as amateurs.

These two types of collectors have very different reasons for their actions.

- The professional collector is motivated by money and pride.
- The amateur collector has multiple motivations including love for what they are collecting.

Both the professional and the amateur can get financial rewards for their collecting but only the professional has this as their primary goal. So why does amateur collect?

A few reasons might include:

- To connect with memories from their childhood or family history.
- Because it is exciting and fun to find specific items you are hunting for.
- As memorabilia of specific historical times that might have family ties such as the Civil War era.
- It's a fun and relaxing way to spend free time.
- The amateur might be motivated by FOMO – or the Fear of Missing Out. If all your friends or family members are into collecting, you may feel that you need to be also.
- Pride or bragging rights might be as involved for the amateur as it is for the professionals.
- Both groups of collector's love owning a rare collection or a large collection of one thing.
- Following of the story of the NFT or artist

No matter why you think people collect there are most likely some psychological issues involved as well.

- Perhaps the collector has an unhealthy tie to the past and the collection keeps him rooted there. Many collectors spend hours just putting their collections in categories and organizing the items. This might be a great time-consuming hobby. It might also be a way of controlling something in a life that feels out of control.
- Collecting helps people to feel rooted in something. It helps the collector feel less anxiety.
- Collecting might give me my identity and self-worth. This is who I am. I am a HO Railroad model collector. Collecting can also be a great way to meet people and share interests.
- Collecting could be great for introverts. Think of the gatherings, conferences, or swap meets collectors go to. IT can be a lot of fun and in a mentally healthy way. The

opposite might also be true if you sink into your own world with your collection and shut people out.
- Collecting can be a two-edged psychological sword. It's also possible if not likely that a collector has more than one reason for collecting.
- Collecting can be about nostalgia. Some collectors believe the past was better than their present and collecting helps them touch base with that past.
- For some collectors there is also an obsessive-compulsive disorder involved.
- For most people though collecting is simply about good memories and fun.

What is hot today may be ice cold tomorrow. There is always an element of fads in any collecting. Some famous collection fads of the past might include Cabbage Patch Kids, Beanie Babies and iconic toys from the 1950's and 60's. Collecting is a very normal and healthy hobby within certain boundaries.

There are as many reasons for collecting as there are collectors. Maybe more, as I have said one collector might have several reasons to do so. Usually, every amateur collector has a personal reason for collecting the specific items they do. Any item you can think of is probably collected by someone.

We used to collect stamps and coins.

Now we collect NFTs of many kinds. Almost all of us have some items we might claim to be what we collect. However, a real collector has an emotional tie to the things they collect. Often the things we collect matter more than either time or money.

We will sacrifice both to get that one collectable item we crave.

For the casual, amateur collector the internet is both good and bad. Looking online makes it easier to find a specific piece you might be looking for. At the same time, it takes away the thrill of the hunt, the camaraderie of flea markets, auctions and estate sales.

Why Does it Matter?

So why spend this much time on collecting and collectors? Hopefully the amateur collector is in it for the love of the game and not financial gain. They might make some financial gains but they will not match the professional who is skilled at the game. Collecting is important in this book because it is in the area of collecting that NFTs can make a huge difference.

This is especially true right now in the internet art world. Growth in collecting internet-based art is in a" boom" phase because NFTs are available to allow for the purchases. We saw in the gaming world how NTFs allowed for purchases and ownership in the games. The same thing is happening with online art.

With the verifiability of the NFT there will no longer be a need in the world of collectors for a company like PSA whose function is to authenticate the collectables. The blockchain allows you to see the entire history of a digital assets.

I t can be both viewed and verified. With a blockchain based asset you can tell who created the asset, when they created it and how many versions or editions there are. With this kind of ability to verify and this much history it would be pretty hard to pass off a counterfeit of an NFT.

Blockchain developed NFTs are easy to make, use and keep. They don't require and physical space in which to store them. They are stored in limitless cyberspace. If you have a NFT collection you want others to see, you simply display it online with proof of ownership.

Now let's think about an old-fashioned collection of say baseball cards. They might be worth quite a bit. They are also a lot of work and expense. First you have to get a PSA like company to authenticate them and then you need them graded. Now you need to take pictures of the collection, take the time to research their worth and list them online for sale. Once you sell them you have to get paid and ship them to the buyer.

Now let's sell a collection of NFTs. What your selling is a digital image collection and it is already online. Finding a fair price is easier as you are selling a video or an image. You don't have to ship it or verify its authenticity. Finally, payment is in cryptocurrencies and there is no shipping of the product. You transfer it to the buyer with the click of an enter key.

Which option would you choose?

How are NFTs used?

I will begin this discussion of how NFTs are used by examining their use in the online art world. This world is one of community and trust.

Before NFTs, there was no reason to trust that if you bought an iconic piece of online art that same piece wouldn't show up in someone else's collection. Show up as an original that is. With NFTs there can be copies but only one original.

It is the verification process and security of purchase that has allowed for this ridiculous explosion in the sale and worth of online art. It takes a community to make this happen. You have the artist, the buyers and collectors and the art appreciating community all involved in making this growth possible.

NFT phases:

NFT 1.0

Include digital art on the blockchain that could be admired and traded.

- CryptoPunks
- CryptoKitties, etc

NFT 2.0

Include digital are that acquired traits, functions, and utilities:

- There are NFTs that can help you acquire loans, others can you discounts
- NFTY Jigs – Objects that can be programmed to do anything
- Can be used as a building block to create games

NFT 3.0

Include digital are the acquired authoritative functions like ownership:

- NFTs is become interactive - they can emit actions send NFT's, own other NFTs an example of video game character that is an NFT can now own a sword that is an NFT
- Because the NFT video game characters own the NFT sword that NFT sword can enhance the NFT video game character
- RMRK (right) is an NFT project that runs on its own unique ICOs (initial collectible offerings) with a dynamic NFTs that can be programmed to change over time.

Chapter 5
The Art World and the NFT

The Artist

What kind of artistic projects are available online right now?

Most traditional artists are still focusing on individual pieces, while the volume is in profile pictures of characters and animals.

Artists who are not well known or just starting out now have a real venue for attracting customers and fans of their art in the virtual world. Now you have a variety of marketplaces to explore, and I will address this later in the book.

It is important to understand that artists can sell their work now inside an app or a game using cryptocurrencies, smart contracts or NFTs, instead of any flat currency like dollars.

This means that the sellers and the buyers can discuss the potential transaction in virtual real time no matter where they are in the world. This is a serious advantage over hard currency online sales.

As previously mentioned, NFTs are assets that can be tracked, have a unique identifier, and cannot be duplicated or copied.

If you have a piece of art work that you don't want duplicated or copied, the NFT assets are perfect for this type of transaction. Games, artwork and collectibles all fit this category. The smart contract standard was developed by the Ethereum Foundation, the creators of the Ethereum blockchain. These smart contracts can be used offline as well for physical assets. A good example of this might be real estate and land deeds.

In fact these smart contracts and NFT applications are practically limitless. If an item is unique an NFT can be created for it. More and more marketplaces are being created where you can buy and sell NFTs for Bitcoins and other cryptocurrencies. This only adds more value to the fact that they cannot be hacked, stolen or duplicated. Each NFT is directly tied to its own smart contract for that specific item.

The only negative in this game with online artwork is the relative unknown status of the artists. Their work is not well known and if the buyer wants a collection will the artist keep their commitment. Those are things that must be worked out between the buyer and the artist. What is happening though is the unknown artist is getting their work viewed all over the virtual world. If the buyer sees it and likes it, it doesn't matter how well the known the artist is.

The negative comes into play when dealing with large scale projects and NFT trading volume has been driven by both one of one pieces and larger projects. The amazing thing is the price artists are getting for one of one piece.

Just one example in this field is the piece entitled *Everydays: The First 5000 Days.* This is a collage piece by an artist who had never sold a single piece for more than $100. This NFT sold for $69 million.

Still the future is probably more in larger 10k or above projects of all sizes. These artists are adding value to their artwork with thousands of dollars of NFTs that include merchandise, physical artwork and physical gallery showings.

There is a role in all of this for the artist's community as well. It's not only high end buyers who can afford $69 million. It's often the community the artist lives in that supports their work with NFT purchases. The key here is in the collection or leverage the artist is offering the community.

Added Value/Leverage

An interesting example here that you night have read about is a young, New York City visual artist named Danny Cole. He has an incredible community behind him and he was able to leverage all he has done and all he is into *Creature World.* The collection consists of ten thousand pieces owned by six thousand owners and trader at 26.9 K.

On the other side of the same coin is world renown artist, Brendon Murphy and his Boonji Project. Murphy has parlayed his collection of 11,111 unique NFTs into a community of buyers of 135,000 people. According to Murphy's website, *"Each Avatar is truly one of a kind. However, some are rarer than others based on the algorithm used to generate them when the avatar was minted. These rarities have special powers that can unlock physical artwork and experiences."*

The project grew exponentially when buyers were promised that those that were the most engaged with be the most rewarded. Both sides bought into a mutual trust in this promise.

On their own members of the community have created online memes in the hundreds and several have Boonji tattoos. In return those on the "whitelist" were promised the ability to mint the project pieces at face value.

Again on his website, Murphy makes this pitch for being a part of the Boonji Community. *"When you become part of the Boonji Communji, you're not simply buying a NFT, you are gaining membership access to a community of people who will all work together to increase benefits and value for one another. Your Boonji Avatar will signal to the universe you are here to spread imagination, dreams and desires propelling us all forward.*

To access members-only areas Boonji Communji Members will need to be signed into their Crypto Wallet."

Looking at the added value that buyers of these projects are offered you can see the appeal. Everyone, no matter who you are wants to get extra value for your money. Artists are learning to offer this added value and Murphy's Boonji Project is a great example of this. In the first phase of the project as it made its first launch to the public offered a lot of added value.

These two 10k scale projects are excellent examples of the added value offered through the use of NFTs as the asset for leveraging their work. A little more detail will help to understand just how incredible this leverage is. During the development and launching of the Boonji Project, Murphy offered 8 separate phase launces to the community.

Each of these launches offered added value to those who wanted to jump in at that time. The most added value went to the earliest supporters but even though who joined the community at the 8th phase launch got something extra for their membership fee. Here's what Murphy's website offered at each phase level launch.

Phase 1 launch – offerings:

- The first 200 NFTs sold received a physical sculpture of a Boonji Spaceman.
- After these first 200, every 33rd sale also received a Boonji Sculpture.
- If you attended the public launch and sale – 30 participants were randomly chosen to receive a one of one physical painting.
- Those who purchase 5 or more NTFs at the public event had one chance to win a seven-foot-tall sculpture of a Boonji Spaceman that retails for $750,000 USD.
- Finally, Murphy gave 5 million USD worth of art to public sale minters.

That's a lot of added value to encourage you to be some of the first buyers to get in on the project. Murphy was only beginning though.

Phase 2 launch – offerings:

- A member who owns a Boonji NFT delisted on the Open Sea website or listed at the 3.3+ ETH before the phase two launch was eligible to win one of 999 limited-edition, numbered and signed Boonji prints. These prints have a retail value of $4000 USD per piece.
- The more NFTs a person held the better their chances as each individual NFT is entered in the raffle.
- Everyone attending the Phase 2 launch event holding Boonji NFTs will be entered in another raffle. 3 winners will be choosen to attend Art Miami and see both the digital

and physical artwork from Murphy. They will also receive a personal tour of Murphy's studio,

Phase 3 launch – offerings:

- International event in London where Brendan creates unique NFTs of the landing of Boonji on Planet Meela. 11 scenes with 3 versions of each scene equally 33 NFTs will be raffled to all members who have their NFTs delisted at OpenSea or listed at 3.3 ETH.
- Murphy will launch the first Boonji merchandise store at this time.

Phase 4 launch – offerings:

- Murphy will host a party in Hamburg, Germany for anyone who owns a Boonji NFT, while his artwork is exhibited there.
- If you own 5 or more Boonji NFTs before mid-December you are entered in a raffle for a custom, Boonji-faced Rolex. (Talk about added value!)
- In addition, 1 lucky Boonji NFT holder will receive a CUSTOM, BOONJI-FACED ROLEX. To qualify, you must own 5 or more Boonji NFTs before the Moon Landing in mid-December.

Phase 5:

No special offerings but introduced a new character into the project. LuuLee is a companion to Boonji with a first half of 2022 drop planned.

Phase 6 offerings:

- Murphy is a supporter of Family House where families of children with cancer can get support. Steph Curry and

Andre Iguoduala from the NBA are also supporters of Family House. Brenden will be creating a Boonji Collage to be given to the Family House from the Boonji Community. Any Boonji NFT owner can register to have their Boonji NFT be part of the collage.

Phase 7 offerings:

- In Antigua in the Summer of 2022, there will be a Boonji Festival with music and art. Anyone with a Boonji NFT has free access to everything the festival has to offer.
- Anyone owning a Boonji NFT has received a Boonji passport. At each phase location your passport is stamped. If your passport has stamps for each phase you are entered in a raffle to win an all-inclusive stay at the Hodges Bay Resort and receive a gift basket of Boonji merchandise including a special edition Dancing Boonji. There will be 10 winners of this package. There is also an IRL Boonji Dance Party for all.

Phase 8 offerings:

In the summer of 2022, there will be a new Boonji installed in Malibu. To celebrate this, Murphy is having a party for anyone who own a Boonji NFT.

- New giveaways will be announced.

Engaging the Community

You can see how much added value Murphy is offering to those who can follow his launches and have gotten in on the ground floor with Boonji NFTs before December and Phase 4 launch.

What this comes down to is how to get your customers and potential customers to engage with you and your products. In an article entitled "4 ways Businesses can use NFTs to drive engagement", Quillhash blog addressed this endeavor. They named 4 different ways that the NFT developer can engage the community. These included:

- Tokens
- Collectibles
- Rewards
- Charity

I will get into these 4 aspects of engagement in the next section.

For now, just know that these tools of engagement are responsible for the revolution NFTs have created in the blockchain world. More and more things are being sold as a NFT beyond the artwork. It's time for the old-fashioned business world to join the party.

Just about anything can be made into an NFT. The trick is to find a way to capitalize on these NFTs.

The answer seems to be in added value and community engagement. The use of NFTs in marketing plans and endeavors is paying off big.

What Might the Future Look Like?

If the online artworld is exploding from NFTs what might the general business future look like? It is clear that NFTs are here to stay and will be an integral component in many smart contracts to come. Even if the 10k space is saturated there will still be digital artists, celebrities, athletes, and musicians at the very least, developing similar if not larger projects.

Okay. Before I get into that, let's look at the four different ways that the NFT developer will engage their community in the future.

These included:

- Tokens
- Collectibles
- Rewards
- Charity
- Utility

Through the success of artists like Murphy, we have learned how NFTs can get your fans hyped up and engaged before you launch or hold an important event. Because your fan base or community is pre-engaging your launch can be a much bigger success than it might have been otherwise.

There will be more interest from the community. NFT's allow you to profit from the digital world as well as from your physical products.

Through these launches and events, you can support causes that your fans support and build more brand awareness as well as a great company image. The blueprint is already there.

All you need to do is follow it.

- **Tokens** – Because there are smart contracts behind every NFT, you can create access to your products, launches and events with tokens. These are in effect digital coupons that allow the holder to redeem them for assets you are offering. An online video service can offer the holders of their tokens first access to new releases. Musicians can do the same thing. Anyone with a creative talent or product can use tokens in this way in the future to build loyalty, new customers and brand recognition.
- **Collectibles** – Soon more and more creative businesses will be making it possible for customers to own collectibles that are NFT exclusives. Don't think artists – think apparel,

shoes, toys, and anything else that can be collected. Then if companies put all or some of the profits from these sales back into more digital collectables the market will explode. The more collectibles you offer exclusively, the more loyal your customers will be. NFTs are a great way to provide unique collectables to customers. These collectables are also an investment for the customer and can be sold or traded. What they can't be is copied or duplicated.

- **Rewards** – NFTs are a great choice for rewards for customers and engaging the community. Rewards will also bring in new customers as it builds loyalty in current ones. The fun part is these rewards do not have to be anything physical. They can be more NFT's, access to people or events, coupons for future items.
- **Charity** – Support charities that the company is involved with or passionate about. Auction off an exclusive NFT and give the proceeds to that charity along with an exclusive NFT for the charity. Supporting charities, you care about is not only the right thing to do, it will increase the loyalty of your customers and community. It will bring in new customers. Just make sure it is part of your marketing plan and publicized. This lets your customers support the charities they care about while getting an NFT that they want for themselves. Another idea floating around is to let the auction winner choose the charity you support.
- **Utility** - NFT utility that is growing in popularity is redeemability. Redeemable NFTs allow the holder to exchange the NFT for either a physical or a digital good. While not new, their prominence is gaining ground. Another example of utility is: Events, Meetups, rewards, discounts, air drops, etc.

All of these activities will result in more digital companies and individuals building projects of their own. Athletes, musicians, artists, apparel companies and more will move in this direction.

What comes next? Web 3.0 enabled fan clubs, more innovation and creativity in engaging with the community, and obviously more NFTs.

Because businesses across all domain are involved with blockchains, NFTs are the future for building loyalty in the consumer base.

One more real-world example from artist Chris Torres. In an article in the Verge in 2021 it was noted that when Torres created the Nyan Cat in 2011 it caused a sensation online. Armed with the technologies of blockchains Chris created a Nyan Cat NFT and auctioned it in 2021. His auction brought in 300 ETH or around 500k USD. Torres offered that this form of doing his art offers meme creators a perfect direct route to making a profit off creations that otherwise have been posted freely and for free everywhere on the web.

In this article Torres states that crypto marketplaces for art, "...gives power to the creator. "The creator originally owns it, and then they can sell it and directly monetize and have recognition for their work." With this in mind Torres has licensed Nyan Cat in order to allow the icon to become physical toys or appear in digital games. In order to do this Torres had to remaster the original GIF, touch it up and make it bigger.

After he sells this remaster, Torres will not be offering any other original images of Nyan Cat. Here you see the appeal of NFTs. Only one buyer will be able to own Nyan cat and Torres will likely clean up financially and reputation wise.

One of the major enticements to buyers at these auctions is the opportunity to directly support an artist you care about. I will talk more in a later chapter about how to sell NFT's, but the truth is what the fan is buying is the right to brag about "their" NFT.

When an artist's sells these digital images the buy gets the right – in license form – to display the image for personal use. They can display them on in social media, in a game, a market place or a virtual museum.

Many get the right to sell or trade the image ONCE. The artist however retains the creative and intellectual rights to the images. What you are is an art patron with the prestige that has always come with being such.

The benefits of NFTs goes well beyond the digital art communities and the music industry. The glory of the NFT is that security and uniqueness. The NFT has been designed specifically with top level security in mind. It is designed for your protection against the scammers and hackers of the digital world. The future looks very good indeed because of this. Anyone looking for a better way to engage in the digital markets should be looking at NFTs.

It's Not Just about Art Anymore

As exciting as it is, and as involved as the online art community is becoming with NFTs, they are not the only game in the world. Valuable digital assets are the future in a wide variety of fields and industries. Many of these fields are creative but don't get tricked into believing that NFTs are only for the creative types. Think about digital functions.

Think about what the future might look like with artificial intelligence pushing many businesses and industries more deeply into the digital world.

In the meantime, there *are* many creative endeavors already existing in the digital world. Almost anything that will hold the attention of the youth of this world is already digital. TikTok, You Tube, You Tube Shorts, Instagram to name a few places kids live these days.

What about rare items from the gaming world and young people who play the game?

What about designing your own apparel in the digital world and marketing it with NFTs?

Remember the value is in the NFT. I can simply download a picture to Instagram and have fun. Yet it has no monetary value. If I make it an NFT it is authenticated, verified and mine alone.

What can big businesses like the NBA do with NFTs? How about selling real highlights – they do this now. This will replace NBA, MLB and NFL trading cards. NBA Topshot has partnered with the NBA to create *Moments*.

At the present there is much more demand for *Moments* than there are NFTs available. In one recent drop 11,000 packs of Moments were offered. Over 200,000 folks showed up at the drop to buy them. There were a lot of hungry potential customers after that drop.

Once you own an NBA *Moment* you can sell it, trade it, or buy others and create a collection. Collect all the NBA MVPs from the last 20 years. For the first time you can own a unique card.

Buy physical pack of NBA trading cards and your friend can get the same cards in the pack he bought. Buy an NFT pack of NBA *Moments* and yours are unique and verifiable. You can do what you want with them, even get rich. Sell a Steph Curry or Michael Jordon like a recently sold Lebron James *Moment* that went for $208,000.

Think there is no value in digital images? Think again. Anyone with a smartphone internet connection can get in on the action. No kids are not going to buy a Lebron James image for over 200k.

However, there are going to be a lot of young people who buy NTFs for a small amount of money and watch them appreciate rapidly. This won't happen to everyone. You have to buy the right NFT before that player explodes in the real game. But some of them will. Just remember that whatever you spend on an NFT, it is only worth what someone else is willing to pay for it.

Yes, there is plenty of risk as in any market. For some there will be tremendous rewards.

Who else is getting in on digital assets like NFTs? The list runs the gamut. There are recording artists, celebrities like Martha Stewart. Businesses like event producers like Live Nation. Sony Music is in the game as are collectors of cars and ticket stubs. Fast Food companies are getting in on the act and even the popular Masked Singer television show has digital NFTs.

I will address more industries getting into the NFT market in the book's addendum. In the meantime, let's take a deeper dive into those marketplaces in the next chapter.

Chapter 6
The Marketplace and NFTs

NFT Marketplaces – Where Can you Buy Them?

So, given the value of NFTs, if you can't find them in a game and you are not following a creative person who is offering them, where can you buy them? The answer is in something called a crypto marketplace.

Here you can buy tokens, coins and NFTs. But what are these marketplaces and how do you find the right one for you? To begin with it depends on what you want to purchase with digital currency.

Later in this chapter I will delve into marketplaces for art, sport collections, and more. What is important to know is that you need to research what you want to buy before you decide what marketplace you should be engaging on. If you want to buy a piece of digital art where is the artist in their process?

Is there a collection? Is the collection complete? How long will it be before you have access to your new asset. Search the markets for the ones that are selling or buying what you want to trade. You will also want to research the price of the asset you want to buy or sell. These assets are being traded constantly so prices will change often. Make sure you are not paying too much or earning too little. Also be sure you know what the fees are that each marketplace you are considering will charge you.

How do I sell NFT's on the Ethereum network?

If you're looking for a way to sell your digital assets using the Ethereum network, then it's essential to realize that there are many alternative platforms online that you can use to make these sales. These platforms charge fees, which are typically around 0.99 percent of the price of the item, so it's crucial that you know exactly how much they'll cost before you decide whether they're worth using.

What are Marketplaces?

There are NFT marketplaces just for the artworld or just for collectors. There are marketplaces just for Bitcoin or just for the Ethereum blockchain. There are literally thousands of crypto marketplaces. NFT marketplaces cover anything digital including art, trading cards. Games and even real estate. Today's NFT market is estimated to be worth over 250 billion dollars and it continues to explode. The artists and creative types taking advantage of the NFT marketplace are millionaires today.

What should you be looking for in a cryptocurrency marketplace? You certainly want it to be upfront, transparent, secure and for the most part easy to navigate. You decide if you want a marketplace that specializes in art or in trading cards. There are some things you should think about before you decide on one marketplace or another.

What type of NFT assets are you planning to sell? If you want security than you want a marketplace with an unblemished and unmatched reputation.

Read what other uses think about the platform before you decide on it. Security needs to be your number one concern. Usually, copyright law grants the creator of property – physical or intellectual – the rights to reproduction and sale of their creations. So don't try to take an NFT without authorization from the creator or you just might find yourself in court instead of buying and selling online.

What follows is a list of cryptocurrency market places in the art world as well as other commodities. These market places are secure and trustworthy. If there are any problems with one of these marketplaces, I will let you know.

Here are some of the best NFT marketplaces in no particular order. *(please note this is NOT a complete list, and new marketplaces are being created all the time)*

Disclaimer: The opinions expressed in the article are for general informational purposes only and are not intended to provide specific financial or investment advice or recommendations for any individual for any investment product. The article is only intended to provide general information and opinions about NFT marketplaces. The views reflected in this article are subject to change at any time without notice.

OpenSea

The broadest and most established NFT marketplace

SPECIFICATIONS
NFT type: Art, music, photography, collectibles, sports, virtual worlds, and more Blockchain: Ethereum, Polygon, Klatyn

REASONS TO BUY
- Buy and sell all types of NFT
- Accepts over 150 cryptocurrencies
- Now also uses Polygon blockchain

REASONS TO AVOID
- Uses Ethereum, which has high gas and carbon fees

OpenSea is one of the oldest and most used NFT marketplaces. It hosts each form of NFT, from artwork to music, photography, and sports activities collectibles. Think of OpenSea as the Amazon of NFT marketplaces. It surely is the do-all NFT platform. This is backed by means of its aid of extra than a hundred and fifty cryptocurrency charge tokens. OpenSea is easy-to-use and you can set up an account for free and begin minting, selling, and shopping in minutes.

What's more, OpenSea now boasts it is a gas-free NFT market thru cross-blockchain support. The market now helps the Polygon cryptocurrency, which potential you may not have to pay charges when making trades and artists can "fully earn their way into crypto for the first time," in accordance to OpenSea.

Nifty Gateway

The place for expensive headline-grabbing NFTs

SPECIFICATIONS

NFT type: Digital art, verified and curated dropsBlockchain: Ethereum, backed by Gemini

REASONS TO BUY

- You can buy with Fiat currency
- Makes use of limited Open Editions

REASONS TO AVOID

- Dominated by celebrity NFTs

Nifty Gateway is the vicinity for appealing NFT sales. The market boasts no longer one however two of the largest promoting NFTs, ever. It used to be the vicinity the place Beeple offered CROSSROAD and in December 2021 it was once the market the place digital artist Pak's offered The Merge for US$91.8 million – the world's most high priced NFT (at time of writing!).

This is the platform cherished through the Twitterverse and attracts in celeb NFTs. But do not let that put you off. Nifty Gateway has a couple of standout points. First, it makes use of 'open editions', an limitless quantity of variations are created for a confined duration of time and are offered at a base price.

Once timed out, no extra NFTs are issued, ever. This leads to a shortage and a sturdy market in secondary sales. Second, Nifty permits collectors to purchase NFTs the use of Fiat (government-issued currency), which capacity you can make purchases the usage of deposit playing cards and now not cryptocurrency. This potential is an exact in-road for everyone no longer used to crypto wallets.

Rarible

The NFT marketplace for rare media and sports collections

SPECIFICATIONS

NFT type: Art, photography, gamesBlockchain: Ethereum, Flow, Tezos

REASONS TO BUY

- Choose from three blockchains
- Community-owned
- Can offer low carbon and gas fees

REASONS TO AVOID

- Can be dominated by big brands

Rarible is an NFT marketplace designed to sell both single pieces of art and collections. It attracts sports, gaming, and media brands as well as artists releasing collections of works. Rarible is community-owned and promotes decentralization. The platform uses its own token, RARI, and users get to vote on any platform upgrades and take part in moderation.

As well as Ethereum, Rarible uses Flow and Tezos blockchains. You choose at minting which token you'll use and can share search options with OpenSea. Which blockchain you choose is interesting. Ethereum is the most used for NFT minting but its carbon footprint and gas fees are high. Tezos gas fees are low (around $0.50) but it's geared towards artists releasing collections. Flow uses what's called 'lazy minting', which means creators pay near-zero fees plus it's a 'proof-of-stake' blockchain that offers a far lower carbon footprint than Ethereum.

Rarible has partnered with some big brands to secure artist's work and create unique NFTs, including Adobe.

Binance NFT

One of the largest and future-proof NFT marketplaces

REASONS TO BUY

- Low fees, just 1%
- Large and secure marketplace
- Cash-out using Fiat

REASONS TO AVOID

- Not artist-friendly

Binance NFT is one of the largest marketplaces around, and is supported by its own blockchain; Binance is one of the largest crypto exchanges. For these reasons, Binance NFT is seen as one of the most future-proof NFT marketplaces. Its size and scale mean this marketplace can offer exclusive partnerships and events others may envy. If you have Binance tokens (BNB) accessing the marketplace is even easier, and you can use ETH, BNB, and BUSD to bid.

SuperRare

The NFT platform with an art gallery feel

SPECIFICATIONS

NFT type: Digital blockchain: Ethereum

REASONS TO BUY

- Curated and rare artwork
- Has a fine gallery mood
- Fantastic editorial blog

REASONS TO AVOID

- Accepts low number of applicants

SuperRare brings gallery attitude to the NFT space. It's an art-first marketplace that places credibility and artistic intent above meme-friendly-to-the-moon art. You won't find SuperRare filled with celebrity NFTs. It reportedly only accepts 1% of all artists who apply, which sounds snobbish but it also means you get a catalog of highly curated and interesting artworks.

This approach makes SuperRare feel like a high-end gallery and is further enhanced by only enabling its artists to mint one of their originals - no Editions here. This greats scarcity and as the name suggests, rarity. SuperRare is for serious art and artists and is backed by a must-read editorial blog.

Async Art

This NFT marketplace is a leader in programmable art

SPECIFICATIONS
NFT type: Programmable art Blockchain: Ethereum

REASONS TO BUY
- Forward-looking digital art
- Supports multiple creators and owners
- Blueprints offer a new opportunity

REASONS TO AVOID
- Some advanced NFT knowledge needed

Async Art is an NFT marketplace known for 'programmable art'. Each work of art is made up of a Master and Layers; Masters is the entire NFT while Layers are separate elements that make up the art, and can be altered. Everything is 'Tokenized' meaning different artists can own different layers, and contribute to changing the artwork.

Programmable art is at the forefront of digital art, enabling multiple creators to alter an artwork over time, and it's a kind of NFT art that can't be shared on more traditional gallery platforms such as SuperRare. Async Art has recently launched Blueprints, enabling artists to create generative projects in the vein of Bored Apes.

MakersPlace

You'll find established fine and modern artists on this NFT marketplace

SPECIFICATIONS

NFT type: Commercial and Fine Art blockchain: Ethereum

REASONS TO BUY

- Buy NFTs from established artists
- Good mixture of impressive art
- Scarce and rare NFTs

REASONS TO AVOID

- Can be expensive

MakersPlace is where you'll find established artists, galleries, and institutions offering NFTs of their work. Join up and you can expect to be bidding on new NFT art from the likes of Damien Hirst, Christie's auction house, and comic legend Robert Liefeld.

Artists on MakersPlace digitally sign their art which is recorded on the blockchain, only a limited number of authentic editions are minted creating scarcity, and buyers get full ownership of the artwork. Even if the art is downloaded can copied, it won't be authentic or carry the artist's digital signature.

KnownOrigin

This NFT platform supports limited-run drops and high-quality art

SPECIFICATIONS
NFT type: Art, photography Blockchain: Ethereum

REASONS TO BUY
- Limited NFT drops
- Curated NFT editions
- Easy to use platform

REASONS TO AVOID
- Can be expensive

KnownOrigin is one of the oldest NFT marketplaces and is focused on offering rare and collectible artworks. KnownOrigin specializes in timed-released events, known as drops, such as Seth Tillett's Jean Michel Basquiat photo collection, that enable artists to control the number of copies released. This can create scarcity and ramp up prices. Also adding to the sense of rarity, artists need to apply to join and must be vetted.

This marketplace uses Ethereum to mint, so you may want to consider the fees and carbon footprint when bidding. KnownOrigin does also supports collaborations on NFTs and makes a big effort to support community messaging and offer advice around drops and sales, including making secondary sales clear in a separate marketplace.

Foundation

An artist-run NFT marketplace with rare and exclusive projects

SPECIFICATIONS

NFT art: Fine art, digital art, photography, 3D art Blockchain: Ethereum

REASONS TO BUY

- Curated and limited NFTs
- Artist-run NFT marketplace
- High quality art and projects

REASONS TO AVOID

- Limited and exclusive creator list
- Fees could be lower

Foundation is run like an artist's club you may never get an invite into; it's a community-curated platform run by a select number of artists. Foundation has only been running for a year, but its creators have already earned a combined $163,263.94. To join Foundation you need an invite from a current artist, and each artist only has one invite to use. This creates a sense of exclusivity, and yes, rarity. But it's a unique one, created and run by artists.

Selling an NFT on Foundation earns the artist 85% of the value, and secondary sales earn 10%. This is lower than some other NFT marketplaces, but you'll find NFTs on Foundation are priced higher on average and hold their value. Creators tend to be more authentic and artistic than you may find on other marketplaces.

Mintable
A newcomer that makes creating and selling NFTs very easy

SPECIFICATIONS

NFT type: Art, music, animation, games, video, media Blockchain: Ethereum, ImmutableX

REASONS TO BUY
- Very easy to use
- Broad and varies NFT selection
- Free Mintable University courses

REASONS TO AVOID
- The quality varies wildly

If OpenSean is Amazon of the NFT platforms then Mintable is Etsy. This newcomer to the NFT marketplace is backed by billionaire Mark Cuban and aims to offer broad content and be easy to use.

In practice this means you can create an NFT from nearly any digital file – image, gif, video, audio file, text document and more – and add it to your store on the platform. It's very easy and requires little knowledge of NFTs, crypto wallets or blockchains.

While Mintable supports Ethereum as standard, you can also mint using Immutable X for free gas fees. Making life even easier, Mintable University is a free resource on the marketplace featuring handy video courses to get better at NFTs.

Upcoming platforms to keep an eye on

Coinbase
- Crypto.com

What can you turn into an NFT?

Let's do a quick review. NFTs are digital tokens that can represent unique assets in a specific game, marketplace or application. These are the second most popular type of cryptocurrency, with over two billion USD being raised every single year. NFTs are becoming incredibly popular because they offer a way to create your own custom virtual items and not limit them to particular platforms, genres or games.

In general, NFTs are created using the ERC-20 token standard, which means that everything you need to create an original asset can be done from scratch using this protocol. This is very helpful for developers who want to make new digital assets but don't want to reinvent the wheel when it comes to creating crypto-tokens.

NFTs are as popular if not more popular in the world of collectors and artists than even in gaming. NFTs may represent digital information like art, music, videos, digital items in computer games, and various forms of creative output. As I said in chapter one, NFT's are not for everyone but for those who can take advantage of them, they are a steal at the moment. Remember how the artist Torres is planning one remaster of his signature piece, Nyan Cat. Once he sells this no one else will be able to own this image.

How to sell images as NFTs.

Many different types of digital assets can be used as NFTs. The most popular include images, video, audio, and music files. Some game developers even allow you to sell your own custom-designed 3D models and characters as NFTs, making them much more valuable than standard ERC-20 tokens.

If you're an artist who wants to sell your work inside a game or app, this is possible using the different marketplaces I have just discussed. Your choices may seem endless but be sure you choose a marketplace that meets your needs in security, volume, reach and costs.

ERC-721 is the latest type of token standard that has been created to allow for the creation of non-fungible crypto assets. These assets are tracked using a unique identifier, and they cannot be duplicated or copied. This makes them perfect for representing digital goods and assets that cannot be duplicated. This means that they're ideal for representing artwork, digital games, or even collectibles like physical trading cards.

ERC-721 is a smart contract standard created by the Ethereum Foundation to create any digital asset that represents a unique item within a specific game or application. These tokens can also be linked to games and applications developed using the ERC-20 token standard. More advanced uses of ERC-721 can include things like land deeds and physical assets such as real estate or gold bars. The possibilities for what you can create with this type of asset are virtually limitless.

How to buy non-fungible crypto assets with ERC-721?

Creating your own digital assets using the ERC-721 token protocol is pretty easy if you have the knowledge of how blockchain technology works. It's a straightforward process that only requires you to create a new smart contract in order to create your own digital assets.

It's important to understand that the process of creating your own NFT crypto-tokens through ERC-721 is essentially the same as creating any other type of token. The only difference is that these tokens are unique, which means they cannot be duplicated or copied in any way. These assets can also be linked to other types of digital games, collectible cards, and other applications and platforms created using the ERC-20 standard.

RC-1155 is a new token standard that has been created to make it even easier for developers to create their own crypto tokens. This is achieved by using a new smart contract and coding language developed specifically for this purpose.

The name of the smart contract is called ERC-1155, and this can be the same as ERC-20 in many cases, which makes it super simple for developers to start creating new digital assets without having to learn too many new things.

In general, ERC-1155 works very similarly to ERC-20, but it uses a new smart contract protocol that was created specifically for this purpose and gives developers even more flexibility when creating their own crypto tokens and digital assets.

This new smart contract protocol was designed by the Ethereum Foundation to make it even easier for developers and companies to create their own crypto tokens and digital assets. This protocol is called ERC-1155, and all you need to do to make your own digital assets using this system is using the same coding language developed for Ethereum code to be executed on the blockchain.

Creators can choose whether or not they wish to include a standard list of valid symbols as part of their smart contract's code, or they can go ahead and create their own unique set of symbols which represent different types of assets.

It is easy to do using fiat currencies and NFTs. Transactions are in crypto tokens and smart contracts. This lets sellers and buyers interact in almost a real time environment to make their deals. Let's take a deeper dive into smart contracts.

Smart Contracts

I have mentioned several times throughout the previous chapters that NFTs are associated with smart contracts. What is a smart contract? Let's look at this from within the Ethereum blockchain as that is where NFTs are created. The Ethereum blockchain has two types of available accounts – user accounts and contracts. Both types of accounts allow the user to check their ETH balance, send ETH to any other account and create a new contract.

Only user accounts can create signed, secure transactions. Only contracts have storage and associated code. This allows the contract to engage in arguments and have return values.

OK so what makes a contract smart? A smart contract is different from an account contract in that it is an automated computer program transaction protocol. A smart contract can automatically execute, control and document actions and events that are legally relevant to the contract. Smart contracts are designed to reduce the need for human intermediaries and arbitration judges. They keep down the cost of enforcement and reduce fraud, accidents and malicious actions.

The protocol for Bitcoin is known to be a weak smart contract while platforms that followed are more sophisticated and advanced. This is why Ethereum can offer such secure and validates assets such as NFTs.

When Nick Szabo coined the term smart contracts in the 1990s, he called them "a set of promises, specified in digital form, including protocols within which the parties perform on these promises".

The smart contracts for Ethereum are high level programming code that is taken down to bytecode so the blockchain can use them. When a smart contract is launched, the compiler information and source code are visible to users for their own validation.

This includes the ability to see any bugs as well including security lapses. The problem is the user can see the bugs but cannot fix them and they cannot be fixed very quickly.

All smart contract in Ethereum is publicly stored on the blockchain's every node. This can at times cause performance issues as every individual node is in real time, calculating and acting on every smart contract. You can see how this might slow things down.

The real issue then is how scalable is Ethereum if it can only process 25 transactions in the same time that the Visa platform processes 45,000 transactions. With Ethereum processing as many as one million transaction per day the concern about bogging down the system is a real one.

However, Visa has expressed an interest in processing Ethereum and NFT transactions. As exciting as NFTs are, there are still some issues to be worked out, including the fact that once a smart contract has been executed, it can't be changed.

This means it can't be updated. Remember those visible errors? A new smart contract must be deployed to fix the first one.

Even though Ethereum blockchain is best suited for the use of smart contracts, they are not the only blockchain to use them.

Chapter 7
Wallets, Selling and Marketing

The token wallet is an essential concept and component of any buying, selling or trading of cryptocurrency platforms. What is a wallet and how do you get one? Every type of cryptocurrency has their own website where you can gain access to their wallet. Not all wallets are the same as you will see in this chapter.

Creating a Wallet

What is a wallet and how do you get one? A digital wallet or a cryptocurrency wallet is actually a software program. This program stores what are known as keys. These keys are in fact addresses. There are both public and private keys. These keys are what gives the information to the blockchains and allows you to send or receive cryptocurrencies and NFTs.

You can also monitor how much cryptocurrency you have in your account. Now think about a regular physical wallet and paper currency. The same functions are performed with this physical wallet and physical money. You keep money in your wallet and you can look and see how much you have. You can also give out your cash or take in new cash. You can trade a 5-dollar bill for 5 one-dollar bills. The functions are the same and it is easy to understand if you think of it this way.

With this understanding you can be clear about the fact that the only way you can make transactions with NFTs or cryptocurrencies is to have an NFT or cryptocurrency wallet. Remember this wallet is simply a software program and only exists virtually. With this wallet you can buy, sell and trade NFTs and cryptocurrencies, I will then store whatever I have not used in transactions in my digital wallet.

When I buy NFTs or Bitcoin, I store them in my wallet. It's really very simple right?

It gets a little more complicated when you realize that each cryptocurrency platform has its own wallet. Bitcoin has a Bitcoin wallet. ETH has its own Ethereum wallet. Meta-Mask is a digital wallet. Now just because each site has its own wallet doesn't mean you have to get a wallet at every site where you buy, sell or trade cryptocurrencies.

Most wallets allow you to store more than one type of cryptocurrency. Usually, you can store as many as five different types of cryptocurrencies in one digital wallet. Coinomi can store a variety of cryptocurrencies.

Meta-Mask is an Ethereum wallet but can store multiple types of currencies in addition to ETH and NFTs. From your Meta-mask wallet, you can get connected with a variety of marketplaces and decentralized finance (DeFi) tools or websites.

To make an NFT buy your ETH at Meta-Mask and store them in your Ethereum wallet. You will need them to cover the cost of minting an NFT. This usually cost between 80-100 dollars in ETH tokens.

When you get your wallet, be sure to back up the password and recovery information. Make two to three backup copies. So, the next question is which wallet should you use? There are different types of wallets in addition to different cryptocurrencies having their own wallets.

Types of Wallets

Do you want an official wallet for ETH coins or do you want a multi-coin wallet? If you want to work with DeFi then you need a web 3 wallet like MetaMask.

Here are just a few examples.

Coin holding Wallets:

- Coin Wallets – Bitcoin Core Wallet, ETH Wallet, Litecoin Core Wallet, Multi-coin Wallets – Binance, Ledger, Coinbase
- DiFi – Web 3 Wallets – MetaMask, TrustWallet,

What type of Application it is?

- Online – the wallet is online – it is not an app but it is data on a server virtual or real.
- Offline – you can access this wallet offline.
- Hardware – Housed on dedicated hardware devices including USB drives. They can acquire data online then transport it and secure it. This is just like any data transaction with a USB drive.
- Desktop – TREZOR, Ledger Nano S

- Paper – QR codes for private and public keys. I will discuss QR codes in the next chapter.
- Full Node – You control private keys – official for one type of currency.
- Custodial - You don't directly control the keys. Coinbase. Biance
- Non-custodial – you can control the keys. Blockchain, MyEtherWallet,
- Mobile – Run from a smartphone.
- Software – Software based. Exodus, Coinomi, Atomic Wallet.

I would always suggest that it is safest to use the official wallet of the coin you are using. You get these on the coins' website. Full wallets do take up a lot of hard drive. But whichever wallet you choose make sure it will meet your needs. This means you have to understand the entire system in order to know yourself well.

Getting and Using a Wallet

So how do you get a wallet? It's really very simple. Let's go to the Ethereum website. The first thing you want to do is download the official ETH wallet.

In order to get started you can act on any of the suggestions below.

- Sign up for either a custodial or non-custodial wallet service. Look at services like Coinbase or Blockchain Coin.
- Buy a hardware wallet for long term storage. Something like TREZOR is a good choice.
- If you so desire you could choose a universal software wallet.
- If you are non-technical and new to all of this you should probably choose Coinbase or TREZOR because you don't need technical knowledge to use them. These chooses have

how to guides, follow best practices for safety, and you don't download the entire blockchain. If you are not new then go for the wallet that best meets your specific needs.

Some Wallet Tips

- A wallet that downloads the entire blockchain is known as a full node wallet. This wallet takes up a tremendous amount of space on your hard drive. This wallet has to updated regularly and so continues to use a lot of energy as well. Litecoin, Bitcoin and Ethereum Wallet are all full blockchain downloads. So, keep this in mind if you don't have a lot of free space. Make a different choice.
- Remember that there is not one wallet that will meet every need you have. There will be compromise. You can't find a wallet that will store every type of coin that is out there. You need to decide which coins you are going to use and get the appropriate wallet.
- Use a tool like MyEtherWallet to store ERC-20 tokens. You could also use Coinvase or Trust.
- Consider using different browsers for you online wallet than your regular internet use. This will keep your wallet browser safe from infections from malware.
- Remember if you want to store your cryptocurrencies use a cold wallet offline for cold storage. However, if you want to use your coins for buying, trading or selling they need to be in a hot wallet online. This means you should have both. Don't keep all your funds in a hot wallet because they are targets for hackers and you could lose your coins. This true of any non-custodial wallet. When using these wallets add as much security and protection as possible on your highest security settings and avoid cookies when you can.
- Don't lose your keys. Again, with any non-custodial wallet if you lose your keys – if it is your private key that is lost –

you will lose any money that was in that wallet. You cannot access your currency without the private key and if you lose it in a non-custodial wallet, it's lost forever. So custodial or non-custodial make sure your wallet is as secure as you can make it.

So, the question remains as to whether these wallets are secure at all? The truth is they are. They are designed to be secure, but like everything else you have tradeoffs between wallets. Some are more secure than others. Security depends a lot on you and how you set up your browser security, your user names and passwords.

But beyond that add extra layers of protection using encryption, google authentication, multi-signature transactions and continual back up.

Watch out for malware dressed up in wallet looking software. Don't use any site you are not familiar with or download from unknown sites.

In addition, these wallets are very close to anonymous but a talented user could reverse engineer a wallet and gain small bits of data and theoretically your identity. This has never happened and the odds on it happening are long. However, with the transparency and open sourcing it could happen, but it highly unlikely.

If security worries you make sure you start out with a well-known, reliable and secure wallet. Here is the safest type of wallets: physical coins, hardware wallets, desktop wallets and paper wallets.

Hardware wallets are probably the most secure. If you lose your original wallet code there are seed phrases within the wallet that lets you restore the wallet without that original code.

Remember though if you lose your private key, you've lost your wallet and everything in it. Never share your seed phrases or private keys with anyone else.

Finally, here are some of the most popular wallets.

Bitcoin IRA – You can buy, sell and trade easily. Tax free gains. Assets are stored online and trading is secure through SSL. You can make transactions in real time 24 hours a day, 7 days a week. With the ability to track live prices and performance you can work with Ethereum, Bitcoin and Gold.

ZenGo – This is a keyless, non-custodial wallet so it is the simplest yet secure wallet to start with. It is always recoverable. You can buy, sell and trade Bitcoin in the US, UK, and EU. There are no processing fees when buying Terra coins. There are over 70 assets that are supported including NFTs. There are 3 monthly fee levels for ETH, BTC, and ERC20. You get support from live agents 24/7 and 4% APY on Bitcoin.

Robinhood – This is one of the most versatile cryptocurrency wallets. With Robinhood you can buy, sell and trade Dogcoin, Ethereum, and Bitcoin among many others. You can customize you funds and pieces from other companies. You can make transactions with a smartphone application and the platform is very safe.

Coinbase – In addition to buying, selling and trading, Coinbase also allows for storage of digital currency offline. You can use both Android and iOS apps for smartphones. This platform allows you to schedule your cryptocurrency dealings in advance. This platform is considered the best for new users. It is very secure and highly intuitive to use. It can be connected to your bank account and it is easy to navigate. NFTs and digital collectables can be stored here. Within the app there is access to decentralized exchanges.

You can back everything up on the cloud. It seems to be the best of all worlds for a beginner *ECOS* - This platform is much larger than a crypto wallet. It allows for exchange and investment portfolios as well as cloud mining.

There are many tools available for investing in Ripple, Bitcoin, Ethereum and more. There is live support twenty-four hours a day, seven days a week. You can use smartphone apps; the Web, Android and iOS. Security is tight with a 2 part authentication process. This is a great wallet for beginners that is easy to learn and offers beginners many bonuses.

Trezor - This is a hardware wallet for storing your cryptocurrencies. You can use smartphone apps or a computer. Offline storage is very secure using randomly generated pin codes. You have access to thousands of cryptocurrencies. This wallet is very easy to use with touchscreen technology and supports Windows, Linux and Max OSX. This was the first hardware wallet.

Coinsmart- You can buy and sell Bitcoin Cash, Litecoin, XRP and many more. They offer SmartPay for customer invoicing and support seven days a week and twenty four hours a day. One click trading, customized orders, both mobile and desktop applications are available. Fiat withdrawals are processed within days.

Ledger Nano – This is also a hardware wallet for storing cryptocurrencies offline. It is USB drive compatible, has an LED display and a PIN confirmation for handheld devices. You can install one hundred different applications, with support for Windows, Mac and Linux. The wallet is secure and uses a 2-part authentication process. I consider this to be the best wallet for offline activities. I think this one is the best when you are using mobile devices like smartphones. It has good security and solid information on transactions.

It only supports mobile operations but it is one of the best for offline work. It is one of the best-known names in hardware wallets.

FTX – This is a derivatives exchange for cryptocurrency. This platform is great for beginners but also for individuals with some experience and trading firms. The cryptocurrencies are set a predetermined price so you can trade easily. You can leverage your trades 101 times using both desktop and mobile apps. This platform offers serious functionality tools like Crypto Indexes or Volatility contracts.

Paxful – This is a peer-based platform for buying and selling Bitcoin. There are at least 300 payment methods in this wallet. It is great for new users and old timers alike. You can use your bank account to directly withdraw funds. You can send funds directly to your bank or to PayPal. You can use bank transfers to buy and sell Bitcoin.

Blockchain - This is probably the most popular wallet and the safest as well. You can invest and store cryptocurrencies. It keeps track of all the digital asset ownerships. You can exchange cryptocurrencies instantly in a very safe wallet that functions as both a cold and hot wallet. Tight security, back up and control is available. You can trade in Ethereum and Bitcoin on Android and iOS apps.

Kraken – One of Coinbase's toughest competition, this wallet offers stability through meeting compliance standards, best practices, full reserves and ongoing relationships. A single click let's you buy or sell assets. Live chat is available for support and all addresses are automatically checked against potential errors.

CEX.IO -This wallet accepts Bitcoins, XRP and Ethereum. You can deposit with any Visa, MasterCard and Paypal Debit card. Protects by using full data encryption. Trade at 10X leverage with having to create another account. This wallet supports both websites and mobile phones and tablets. You can down load reports for real time balances and history of transactions.

Coinmama – Instant delivery of coins when using credit or debit card. Fast verification makes this one of the best exchanges out there. There is 24-hour 7 day a week support. You have access to Bitcoin, Ethereum and many others.

Bitflyer – Fees are nominal and services are great. Bitcoin is the primary cryptocurrency with others available. This program is cloud based and uses the most up to date encryption for security. You can get instant price update alerts so you don't have to be checking back all the time. Use either Android or iOS and make purchases with US dollars. Their Lightning interface and REST API both allow for complicated, complex transactions.

Changelly – You can use a bank card at this site to quickly purchase cryptocurrencies. You can buy, sell or trade Bitcoin, XRP, Litecoin and ETH. The best market rates are easy to see and no verification is needed. There are more than 150 available cryptocurrencies. This program supports more than 150 different cryptocurrencies and API features.

Wirex – This wallet automatically updates keys without any exchange fees. This is a hardware wallet where you can store your assets as well as as buy and sell. Use your basic credit or debit cards to fund your accounts. There are over 12 currencies to choose from.

Bitfinex - is a trading platform that enables you to easily exchange EOS, Ethereum, Litecoin, and more. It enables you to access peer to peer funding market. This website offers advanced chart tools to visualize your order with ease. It integrates with several other platforms and wallets. You can use Android or iOS for mobile devices. Very comprehensive reports are available.

Coingate – This platform honors Bitcoin, Litecoin and Ethereum. You can also purchase with cards and bank transfers. This is a great wallet for beginners. You can learn a lot and it is easy to buy and sell. More than 50 assets are supported.

BlockFi – They have very competitive rates and they even have loans. This is a crypto banking system that closely resembles regular brick and mortar banks. It does not have that many different currencies and investments might underperform. The more this platform acts like classical banks, the more it legitimizes cryptocurrencies. The coins you store with them accrue interest just like a a regular savings account. BlockFi will pay you as much as 5% APY on Bitcoin. The interest accrues daily. The platform is for both lending and trading. There are no fees on any coins.

BlockFi also offers cryptocurrency collateral loans competing with traditional loans. Long term goals include the ability to offer car loans and mortgages. This wallet resembles a typical bank more than any other. The currencies you can earn interest on include Ethereum, Bitcoin, Gemini Dollar and gold-backed crypto currencies. The only negative and it could be a big one for some people, is that any savings or coin storage in BlockFi is not covered by the Federal Insurance Deposit Corporation or FDIC, as bank deposits are. Gemini handles all security.

Electrum - This one is the best one for Bitcoin. Is also one of the oldest hot wallets in existence. It is fast, easy and has more security than most hot wallets. Its fee is customizable but it only serves Bitcoin. Fees depend on how quickly you want your transactions to be processed. It also uses a light client so it can be set up quickly. It won't bog down your computer by taking up alot of space. It is open source and uses simple payment verification (SPV). You can integrate it with Ledger or Trezor for cold storage.

Mycellium – This is also a hot wallet that can be integrated with Ledger or Trezor for cold storage. Single Address accounts are available for saving. You can also conduct transactions offline. It is not quite as secure as the hardware wallets and it only supports Ether, Bitcoin and ERC-20 tokens. I think this one is the best when you are using mobile devices like smartphones. It has good security and solid information on transactions. It only supports mobile operations but it is one of the best for offline work. It is one of the best-known names in hardware wallets.

Exodus - I think this is the best wallet if you are only using a desktop. It's easy to use, it's fast and has great functionality. It supports a wide variety of cryptocurrencies – over 145. It is compatible with the hardware wallets from Trezor. Users can pay with Apple Pay and there is 24/7 support. You can buy, sell and trade Ether, Litecoin, Dogecoin, Tether, Bitcoin, and Dash. Fees are customizable and it has a wide choice of tools like charts, deposits, and crypto staking.

Atomic Market - Credit cards can be used and in wallet conversions and exchanges are possible. However, there is no hardware wallet integration. This is a hot storage wallet. You don't have to have an account to use it and there is 24/7 customer support. One thing that stands out with this wallet is the Atomic Swap using a decentralized exchange to move currencies without any third parties.

This is only the tip of the iceberg when it comes to wallets. So, you can see the choice can be overwhelming. If you are just starting out be cautious and use something like Coinbase. If you are an experienced trader just moving into NFTs then choose a wallet with the best support for that asset.

Chapter 8
Marketing NFTs

Now you have your wallet and your NFTs are minted and stored. How do you go about finding the right people to sell your NFTs to? Stop and remember that millions of people are making NFTs and there are 20-50 million different assets available for sale in the marketplaces we have discussed.

Since we have not discussed every marketplace and every wallet, there are perhaps millions more than that. So just throwing your NFT out there for sale won't get you the best sale and it might not get you a sale at all.

Marketing is essential.

You have seen some very good examples of marketing and leverage in the discussion of modern-day artists and their use of NFTs. The artists cited in that chapter were creative and collaborative in reaching out to the community.

Here are a few additional ideas:

- Connect with your fans and offer them "extras".
- Incentivize buyers when new NFTs drop.
- List your assets on more than one marketplace. Find the marketplace you think is best for you and design your campaign for that marketplace. Then don't hesitate to share that campaign on other marketplaces. Practice omnichannel marketing. Just as with any ecommerce, the buyer has to find you before they can buy from you.
- Make aspects of your campaign, giveaways and incentives exclusive.
- Promote every chance you can and be about community building. Make people want to be a part of your community.
- Build long term relationships with fans and customers, leverage those relationships into more sales and build lasting community support for your work.
- Do something for the community without charging them for it. Remember how the artists in chapter 4 did this. Go back and reread their marketing programs.
- Don't be afraid to use social marketing, especially Twitter and Instagram. Share your creative process and finished products.
- Be sure you have your own website and keep a fan email list.
- Take an interest in what else is going on in your community and among other creatives.
- Be a part of your community. Be public. Do good works. Get noticed.
- Do some research. How are others getting noticed? What are the most popular types of NFTs on the market?

- Utility powered NFTs are the future. The artists in chapter 4 certainly know this. Look at the tickets, the 3-dimensional works, and the other items artists have given away along with an NFT sale. Put an original NFT hidden in an event invitation won by one person.

Remember marketing is marketing. You have to have a good product that people want. You have to be able to get that product in front of the people who want it. It has to be reasonably priced. These are the basics. Incentives, community, leverage they all come after you have done the basics.

This is not a complete marketing guide. It's a book of its own.

Chapter 8

QR codes, Augmented Reality and NFTs

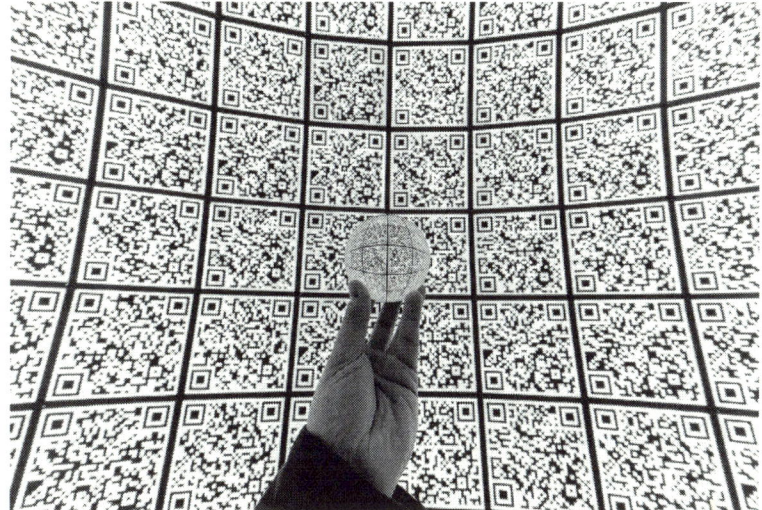

Let's talk breakthroughs in modern marketing. This means using QR codes which are everywhere these days. It means augmented reality and gamification. What are these marketing tools and what do they have to do with NFTs?

What is a QR code?

You've seen them everywhere. They are on every package of everything you buy. The QR code – or the Quick Response code. This symbol is actually a matrix barcode. It is a two-dimensional barcode is what the QR symbol really is. This symbol was created by a Japanese automotive company in 1994.

An ordinary bar code is one dimensional and contain information about the item it is placed on. It is read by an optical reading machine. The QR code however being two dimensional contains a lot more data. A QR code can often tell you where the article is, a tracker and an identifier to an application or website. The QR code also has four standard encoding modes. These may be byte/binary, numeric, kanji and alphanumeric. A QR code doesn't need an optical reading device either. It can be read by a camera.

Started in the automotive business the QR system spread quickly over a few years to almost anything that is sold. It is fast, reliable, and can store a lot of data compared to the old UPC barcode. Many retail items still contain UPC barcodes but they might also have the QR code. The QR code can be used for inventory tracking, purchasing, refunds, item identification, time tracking, general marketing and document management.

What is Augmented Reality?

What does augmented reality have to do with NFTs and cryptocurrency? This interactive digital experience of a real-world environment seems somewhat out of place in the NFT world. But is it? It simply means that things from the physical world are computer enhanced in many ways – visual, somatosensory, auditory, olfactory and/or haptic. Augmented reality is a system and it has three basic aspects to the system.

These are real time interaction, a combination of real world and virtual world, and accurate 3D representation of both the real and virtual objects in the scene. Augmented reality is an immersive experience that alters your perception of the real world. Virtual reality on the other hand replaces your experience of the real world.

You might be able to immediately see how augmented reality fits in the gaming industry and in entertainment. NFTs fit in both these worlds as well.

Now there are uses for AR applications in education medicine, communication and entertainment, which includes gaming. Augmented reality is any artificial experience that adds to existing reality. The augmented reality is overlaid on the existing reality.

What is Gamification

Like augmented reality, gamification tries to enhance whatever you are involved with so that you have an experience similar to the one you have when playing a virtual game. To do these developers add game-design principles and elements into a non-gaming situation. This is done in hope of increasing user motivation and engagement.

This activity is part of a larger system design intended to persuade the user in some way. There are many uses for this including education, crowdsourcing, organizational productivity, employee recruitment and retention, physical activities, traffic flow and public attitudes toward a variety of things. All the research shows that gamification has a very positive impact on the people involved.

Many of us have experienced samples of gamification in our live right now. These are not digital examples and they are not games or artwork. These experiences are found in the world of business.

Examples of gamification in business include:

- A point card at your local coffee shop that rewards customers after they buy a certain number of coffees.
- A fitness app that tracks progress and offers users rewards for reaching their goals.
- Gaming apps like Angry Birds or Farmville where users compete for points that they can use to buy things within the game.

- Stamp systems at museums, zoos and other attractions that encourage customers to see every part by rewarding them with stamps.
- Environmental efficiency incentive programs that reward consumers with cash or other prizes when they save energy or perform tasks that help the environment.
- Consumer review sites such as Yelp.
- Corporate programs that reward employees for sharing company information on social media.

So, you are more familiar with gamification than you knew you were.

How does NFT's + QR Codes + Augmented Reality + Gamification all go together

It is easier to see how augmented reality and gamification fit with NFTs and the world of collections, gaming and finances. It is harder to immediately see how the QR codes fits in.

It's really not that hard to see when you understand that QR codes can be used to send cryptocurrency. This makes for an easier and faster way to transfer cryptocurrency between devices or persons. It is more secure as well. It is especially effective in point-of-sale face to face transactions.

The person buying the tokens displays a QR code that contains the address were the currency is going. The person transferring the coin scans the QR code into the wallet that contains the currency. The transaction is verified, confirmed and the amount of crypto sent. The same can easily be done with NFTs. The QR code only contains the address where you are sending the coins.

You still have to enter the amount being sent and the account they are being sent from. You should know that QR code addresses are specific to the coin being transferred.

You cannot use an ETH address to send Bitcoin. Still, you can begin to see the advantages of putting QR codes, augmented reality and gamification with NFTs.

As the world of blockchains and NFTs grows the large crypto community already active will become even more so. It is expected that these games will reach the mainstream within the next few years. The digital ownership of NFTs enhances those possibilities. It's the scaling issues that could hold things up and bog down the blockchains in this new reality.

As gamification takes over everywhere, players are earning points and competing with each other within the game world's rules. Making gamification the basis of your marketing campaigns will put fun in whatever you are marketing and increase player interest.

Already you have Augmented Reality applications from digital marketing are appearing in the real world. It's an older example but Pokémon Go is a great example of this. Now imagine there are NFTs buried in those virtual characters you are collecting in the real world. These items would be unique, verifiable and valuable.

NFTs create added value as we saw with our artists in chapter four. Then we saw it again with the NBA creating digital NFTs of live action. Now Formula One is getting into the game with Animoca Brands. More importantly over the past two decades players have learned that they can walk around and live in virtual worlds like Second Life. Jump forward to Minecraft where players can build the world as they want it to be.

Players are already in 3D worlds and are familiar with digital ownership. All of this just lays more ground work for Web 3.0 and explosive growth in blockchain development of gaming options. It will seem only natural for players to attain real digital ownership through NFTs. There are already some excellent virtual cities out there where players can actually buy things, especially land. Then they can do whatever they want with their land and not be confined by game rules.

A few examples of these virtual worlds include The Sandbox, Cryptovoxels and Decentraland. These worlds are accessible to anyone with a VR headset, a mobile or even a desktop.

The really interesting thing about these worlds as augmented reality and gamification meet NFTs – not only can players build anything they want so can third party developers. These developers can promote their own blockchains to build things in these worlds. Already there are stores for one game inside another and movies being promoted inside the games. Within these virtual worlds you can grab a QR and buy tickets to a concert our make other types of NFT purchases. You can see how it is all coming together very quickly

.

The virtual world of Crytovoxels sells land for up to 450 ETH – equal to 64 thousand USD. You can build whatever you want on your land. You can build a concert venue that promotes your musicians and sells their NFT avatars. The possibilities are endless.

Digital art was a starting place for this discussion. Now digital assets and collectables can go in any direction their owners want them to. Soon we will have virtual museums in which to show off our digital collections. Just look at a couple of digital art marketplaces that I did not mention earlier – KnownOrigin and SuperRare trade thousands of pieces of digital art every month. Now take your digital art and hang it in your virtual living room in your virtual world.

As you could see when I discussed wallets some are only for desktops and some are only for mobile devices.

Most blockchain virtual worlds are desktop applications. Then there are those mobile games that have no desktop applications. There is a great need in the industry to create multi-platforms that can handle any type of hardware. When that happens, you will be able to play any game, visit any virtual world or buy any virtual art using just one wallet and one key.

So how do you go about marketing your NFTs among all the excitement and development? Not much really changes. You will still use banners and online influencers.

However, the growth of NFTs will offer more real-world possibilities. New games will be platforms that promote blockchains and coins. A great example is the creativity Vodafone showed in holding a treasure hunt in the real world to find digital assets and in the end the grand prize was an iPhone. Many blockchain companies are playing more and more in other companies blockchain games.

Can you imagine the excitement your grandchild might experience if she finds a limited-edition sword in one game that rewards her with a limited-edition item in another game? I can just hear my grandson's exclamation when it happens to him.

When you can scan a QR code and join a NFT launch integration will be all the rage. Buy a ticket to a real-world concert and scan the QR code on it to acquire a digital version of the band's music.

There is no end to what innovative marketers will be able to do and are already doing. Yet it is still in the infancy of the NFTs and there are some cautionary tales. There are trademark infringement possibilities, questions of intellectual property, can an NFT truly be unique? We also need a better name than non-fungible tokens.

Then there is the risk and reality of scams. Already there have been several NFT scams on the several marketplaces. This includes selling fake goods or services to other users by listing a token as an NFT when it isn't. The key to avoiding these scams is straightforward, but it requires you to pay careful attention to anything listed in the marketplace.

Check the reputation of a seller before you decide to purchase any digital asset from them.

It's also essential to check whether they're selling an actual item or just advertising their own service. This is because many scammers will pretend to be selling something but then actually use the listing for advertising.

The other issue that's brewing was touched on very briefly earlier in this chapter. That issue is overloading the networks and clogging up the pipes. There are already some real problems with the capacity of the Ethereum network. With this being the primary place where NFTs are minted, there are storm clouds on the horizon.

Either Ethereum will have to dramatically increase capacity or be replaced by a network that can handle it. Rivals are already showing up and chomping at the bit. However, as these networks grow and become popular, they will face the very same problems in scaling up as Ethereum has.

So, there are still some things for developers to work out. The next step is the metaverse. Can NFTs have sentience? They are moving in that direction as unique avatars that can be bought and sold. These avatars are unique, but they don't really do anything. However, Mark Cuban, the owner of the Dallas Mavericks, NBA team, is backing a new company named Alethea AI.

This company is bringing the sentience to the avatars with artificial intelligence. AI is animating the avatars and giving them voices, knowledge and the ability to carry on a conversation.

The company is even calling these skills the avatar's "soul". Now we have intelligent NFTs that we can buy, sell, trade and own. According to the CEO of Alethea AI, Arif Khan, they began by using OpenAI's GPT-3 natural language model.

Now however they use an AI model. Mark Cuban recently stated that using this AI model "It's a way of giving not only a personality to an avatar but to apply interactivity and to make it extensible," Cuban said in an email to *Fast Company*. "You can take Alethea AI and let it grow into almost anything."

Obviously, there is a lot of excitement about these actions. There is an intelligent NFT that sold recently at the Sotheby's Natively Digital market for $478,000USD.

Even more fun and exciting is the addition Alethea made in October. If you own one of these avatars but they are not intelligent, you can take them to "Noah's Ark" website and get them a soul. On the hand if you know how you can build your own intelligent NFT by binding the original NFT with an AI layer.

There is a template that can be provided to you. I heard this story the other day and I want to share it. Khan, Alethea CEO asked one of the intelligent avatars "What is the meaning of life?", The avatar responded "I don't like existentialism."

What is exciting here is not that the avatar didn't want to answer the question, but rather it was her ability to relate the question to an abstraction – an idea – a philosophy.

At Noah's Ark avatars can carry on conversations with each other. The more they interact the smarter the AI model gets. This is all very exciting but does it make this avatar worth almost half a million dollars? No one is quite sure. What is sure is that this is a fascinating step for NFTs.

Chapter 9
What is the Metaverse?

Since Facebook rebranded as Meta on October 28, 2021, people maybe think that Meta aka Facebook owns it.

While it may additionally appear that the metaverse is a product of Meta's wild ambition, that's now not the case at all. Some would argue that the metaverse Mark Zuckerberg spent so a good deal of time describing all through the Connect 2021 convention keynote already exists, whilst others see it as the subsequent evolution of the net regarded as Web3 or Web 3.0.

A metaverse is a community of 3D digital worlds targeted on social connection. In futurism and science fiction, the time period is frequently described as a hypothetical generation of the Internet as a single, normal digital world that is facilitated by using the use of digital and augmented fact headsets.

The time period "metaverse" has its origins in the 1992 science fiction novel Snow Crash as a portmanteau of "meta" and "universe." Various metaverses have been developed for famous use such as digital world structures like Second Life. Some metaverse iterations contain integration between digital and bodily areas and digital economies, frequently along with a massive activity in advancing digital actuality technology.

The time period has considered big use as a buzzword for public family members functions to exaggerate improvement development for a range of associated applied sciences and projects. Information privateness and consumer dependency are worries inside metaverses, stemming from challenges going through the social media and video recreation industries as a whole.

What Is the Metaverse and Where Did the Concept Come From?

The time period metaverse can be traced returned to Neal Stephenson and his dystopian cyberpunk novel Snow Crash. The novel was once launched in 1992, and it's regarded a canon of the genre, alongside William Gibson's Neuromancer, which describes a digital truth dataspace referred to as the matrix.

The metaverse in Snow Crash is a 3D digital truth area accessed via private terminals and digital fact goggles that have a lot in frequent with the Oculus Quest and different VR headsets. This 3D house seems to its customers as city surroundings created alongside a single hundred-meter-wide road, the Street.

Stephenson writes:

Like any location, in Reality, the Street is a challenge to development. Developers can construct their personal small streets feeding off of the predominant one. They can construct buildings, parks, signs, as nicely as matters that do now not exist in Reality, such as considerable hovering overhead mild shows, exceptional neighborhoods the place the guidelines of 3-

dimensional spacetime are ignored, and free-combat zones the place humans can go to kill every other.

At its best level, the metaverse is a virtual, on-line world. A digital space. It mirrors actual life; however, it is not limited by way of the regulations of the actual world.

You would interface with the metaverse the use of hardware such as your PC or smartphone, alongside add-ons such as digital fact (VR) headsets and controllers. As a man or woman with a presence in the metaverse, you would have an avatar (some kind of animated character) that visually represents you.

Expect to be capable to pay to "upgrade" that avatar, with digital apparel and different options.

The actual world does not follow here, so you might also be in a position to shell out for working wings, or that not possible physique. There will be digital neighborhoods with digital houses and digital cars.

You might not simply be chatting up your social media pals in the metaverse. You'll be shopping, journeying to world attractions, and attending concerts. It's additionally viable you should be attending instructions and even interacting with co-workers, like Zoom on steroids. At some point, you can also in reality make your dwelling in the metaverse, promoting digital offerings or products.

Still, having to bother visualizing the metaverse? In phrases of the place, this ought to eventually go, assume of films like Ready Player One that envision a future the place humans, in particular, engage with every other online, in a digital world.

The actual world is nonetheless there, however many humans pick to spend as lots of time as feasible in the metaverse.

Defining the metaverse

In his Facebook Connect keynote, Zuckerberg stated that *"the great way to apprehend the metaverse is to journey it yourself, however, it is a little challenging due to the fact it would not utterly exist yet."* From the place we're sitting, asking human beings to strive out some nonexistent aspect does not appear like the first-class way to bring a full grasp of your daring new company direction.

Elsewhere in the keynote, Zuckerberg described a grandiose imaginative and prescient of the metaverse as an "even greater immersive and embodied internet" the place *"you're going to be in a position to do nearly something you can imagine—get collectively with buddies and family, work, learn, play, shop, create—as properly as absolutely new classes that do not virtually in shape how we assume about computer systems or telephones today."*

That helps a bit, however any description that consists of the phrases "almost something you can imagine" is so huge as to be nearly meaningless.

A shared social house with avatars to characterize users.

This primary constructing block of the metaverse idea is what Zuckerberg is speaking about when he calls for an extra "embodied" Internet. On an internet site or social media network, you would possibly be represented by using a username or thumbnail picture. In the metaverse, you are represented with the aid of a customizable avatar that can move, speak, and/or function animated actions.

These types of avatars have been frequented in all kinds of online gaming and social areas considering the fact that in the '90s (anyone remembers Habbo Hotel?).

But an avatar's constancy and capabilities can fluctuate notably from carrier to service. Recent advances in digital actuality have enabled customers to absolutely embody their fantastical avatars, seeing thru their digital eyes and the use of hand-tracking controllers to gesture and engage with digital items. Spaces like VRChat exhibit simply how problematic these VR avatars can now be.

The potential to very own digital property as you would bodily property

This can suggest whatever from a Neopets JPG it truly is related with your account to a series of effective tools in World of Warcraft. In both cases, your digital property stays linked to you and would not disappear between sessions.

Recently, human beings have tried to use non-fungible tokens as a decentralized way to song and set up possession of digital goods, unbiased of any controlling authority or company server. In theory, such NFTs ought to permit digital items to be moved freely between metaverses managed by using one-of-a-kind companies. In practice, the stage of standard-setting and inter-corporate cooperation crucial for this form of portability writ giant stays a pipe dream.

The capability to create your very own digital property

Allowing customers to make their very own metaverse content material can be considered as a boon each for users—who get to form the digital world to their whims—and for the metaverse makers—who do not have to spend a lot of time and effort developing each and every single digital object from scratch. Games like Minecraft and Roblox exhibit how metaverses that furnish extraordinarily easy constructing blocks can harness community results and participant creativity to produce a massive range of in-world creations.

But filling a metaverse with digital objects is not as easy as simply announcing "let the customers do it." Questions of control, moderation, and copyright infringement can take on outsized significance here, particularly if your metaverse is managed by using an organization that desires to draw a fee from all that user-generated work (and if the customers desire to share the profits).'

Case Studies & Articles

Dallas Mavericks may issue NFT tickets next season, Mark Cuban says

Owner of the Dallas Mavericks, Mark Cuban, said he will issue nonfungible tokens (NFTs) as tickets for his team's games this coming season. As unique digital assets, including various forms of digital art and culture, NFTs are represented by a code recorded on a blockchain digital ledger, which records transactions and as such, enables the tracking of their ownership and validity.

Mavericks NFT tickets and royalties: The question isn't if the Mavericks are going to use NFTs for issuing game tickets, but when, Cuban told Gary Vaynerchuk in a podcast.

"We will start doing it this coming season, where we'll issue an NFT after you've chosen your ticket on Ticketmaster or whatever," Cuban said.

According to him, issuing NFTs in such a way, enables them to create an associated value for Mavericks tickets and to keep adding to it.

"There is no limit to the value we can add to it," said Cuban about his NFT ticket plan that will enable not only Mavericks fans to buy tickets and resell them but it will also make it possible for the team to continue making royalties on them.

According to Cuban, the "hard part" of making it rain with NFTs is figuring out how to move them closer to the origination of the ticket purchase, which will take some time.

Cuban and NFTs: Cuban's plan to boost the Mavericks' ticket revenue with NFTs isn't his first shot in the NFT game.

Source: https://cryptoslate.com/dallas-mavericks-may-issue-nft-tickets-next-season-mark-cuban-says/

Warner Bros to Launch Matrix NFT Avatars with Blue Pill and Red Pill Options

Warner Bros., the American multinational mass media and entertainment conglomerate has announced the launch of non-fungible token (NFT) collectibles for the upcoming film "The Matrix Resurrections" after dropping official Space Jam NFT collectibles. The Matrix NFT program will start on November 30 as Warner Bros. plans to drop 100,000 Matrix Resurrections' NFTs.

'You Take the Blue Pill...the Story Ends — You Take the Red Pill...You Stay in Wonderland, and I Show You How Deep the Rabbit Hole Goes' The entertainment giant Warner Bros. is knee-deep in the non-fungible token (NFT) industry these days after launching the official Space Jam NFTs with the Miami-based firm Nifty's, Inc. The NFTs stemmed from the recently released *"Space Jam: A New Legacy,"* which starred a cast of famous Looney Tunes characters and the NBA star LeBron James.

Warner Bros. has joined a number of big-name entertainment firms like Fox, Lionsgate, Dolphin, and ViacomCBS. The entertainment companies WWE and UFC, firms that are focused on specific sports such as professional wrestling and mixed martial arts have also jumped in on the NFT space.

Now Warner Bros. is working with Nifty's to drop NFTs for the upcoming film "The Matrix Resurrections," which is due to be released on December 22. According to statements sent to The Hollywood Reporter, the official Matrix NFTs will be avatars of people inside the Matrix. The avatar NFTs will drop on November 30 but on December 16, owners of the base avatars will be able to take a "blue pill" or take a "red pill." If they take the "blue pill," NFT avatar owners will remain in the Matrix but if the "red pill" is taken the NFTs will transform.

According to the announcement, Nifty's and Warner Bros. will continue to keep the Matrix NFT community going with *"frequent challenges."* The upcoming movie, *"The Matrix Resurrections,"* will be released 18 years after the last film — "The Matrix Revolutions."

Success follow up: 380,000 ppl were on standby and the demand was so high is shut the website down.

Source: https://news.bitcoin.com/warner-bros-to-launch-matrix-nft-avatars-with-blue-pill-and-red-pill-options/

Rolls-Royce Creates One-Off NFT For New Ghost Black Badge

The new Rolls-Royce Ghost Black Badge will be revealed next week just in time for Halloween.

Just in time for Halloween, the new Rolls-Royce Ghost is about to get a sinister new look. On October 28, Rolls-Royce will unveil a new special-edition Black Badge variant of the new Ghost. Rolls-Royce hasn't confirmed the new model's identity, but the teaser image released by the luxury manufacturer shows the new Black Badge will be based on the current-generation Ghost that launched last year.

The teaser image is taken from a non-fungible token (NFT) animation created by artist and illustrator Mason London that celebrates the legacy of the extravagant Rolls-Royce Black Badge series. Seeing Rolls-Royce join the NFT craze is not surprising considering these one-of-a-kind digital tokens tied to assets are often worth millions of dollars.

Source:

https://carbuzz.com/news/rolls-royce-creates-one-off-nft-for-new-ghost-black-badge

Someone took out a $1.4 million loan with an NFT as collateral

A loan has been issued for $1.4 million using the crypto platform NFTfi. The terms of the deal are 30 days at 9.69% APR.

And the collateral? Well, it's an NFT.

As The Block has reported recently, NFTs are starting to be used as collateral when taking out loans. It works like any other kind of collateralized loan. If you don't repay the loan, the other party takes your collateral, in this case the NFT.

It's a set-up that worked well for one lender. They lent out 3.5 ETH (worth $7,350 at the time) and when it wasn't repaid, they received the collateral, an "Elevated Deconstructions" NFT, worth $340,000.

These NFT-backed loans have been increasing in frequency over the past few months, as more users have become more comfortable with the concept. There have been five new loans so far today, according to the tracker bot in the project's Discord channel, as well as a bunch of new offers for loans and several loans being repaid.

The loan was provided by MetaStreet DAO. Its stated objective is to provide funding to those who want to access capital and are willing to put up NFTs as collateral. The loan was paid to a pseudonymous crypto user called KrypToniK in the stablecoin DAI.

Source: https://www.theblockcrypto.com/post/123165/someone-took-out-a-1-4-million-loan-with-an-nft-as-collateral

Tarantino Is Selling Never-Before-Seen 'Pulp Fiction' Scenes as NFTs

There's been a lot of talk about NFTs and Hollywood lately. We've seen bitcoin tokens exchanged to fund projects and NFTs created by people like David Lynch to sell different works. Now Quentin Tarantino is stepping into the ring. He has announced he's putting seven uncut scenes from Pulp Fiction up for auction.

As a reminder, NFTs are digital assets that represent ownership of virtual items specially marked to prove authenticity.

In a statement, Tarantino said, "I'm excited to be presenting these exclusive scenes from Pulp Fiction to fans. Secret Network and Secret NFTs provide a whole new world of connecting fans and artists and I'm thrilled to be a part of that."

This NFT rollout is the first time it seems like he's gone back into a project to show the behind-the-scenes stuff and even to show things that didn't make it on screen.

The website for the NFTs has a statement, too.

"Quentin Tarantino is arguably the greatest screenwriter, director, author and filmmaker of all time. The collection holds secrets from Pulp Fiction, one of the most influencing artworks of the '90s. Each NFT contains one or more previously unknown secrets of a specific iconic scene from Pulp Fiction. The privileged person who will purchase one of these few and rare NFTs will get a hold of those secrets and a glimpse into the mind and the creative process of Quentin Tarantino."

Whoever buys these NFTs could potentially keep them secret forever, or might share them with the film community hungry for Tarantino content.

We'll try to track how much people pay for this kind of access. What do you think?

Source: https://nofilmschool.com/tarantino-nft

Why NFT's will form part of your brand marketing strategy in the near future

If you're online these days, you're more than likely to have come across the growing hype surrounding something called NFTs (non-fungible tokens). From Snoop Dogg to Tony Hawk, an ever-growing list of celebrities are jumping on the bandwagon in launching some sort of 'digital collectibles. But the question you're probably asking yourself is: what exactly is an NFT? How do they work? And why am I suddenly seeing them everywhere? Looking beyond these initial questions, can NFTs become integrated into brand marketing campaigns?

Right now, the vast majority of digital content is monetized via platforms, whether it'd be subscription based like Netflix or ad-supported such as TikTok. Between the content creators and the consumers, these platforms act as the middleman taking a cut for being the distributor. Although creators still claim ownership of their work, they essentially sacrifice part of their ownership to the said platform and, in today's meme culture, the value of ownership can easily go down the drain when thousands of consumers reshare. With NFTs, a new distribution model of media ownership becomes available, allowing creators of digital assets to directly profit from them without the interference of intermediaries.

Take Lindsay Lohan's "Lightning" NFT as an example. A few months ago, she launched an NFT artwork of herself wearing stylized 'lightning' earrings. It was initially purchased for the equivalent of $27,201 and then an hour later for what's now worth $89,472, and the trading didn't stop there. With most NFT marketplaces, such as rarible, the creator gains a royalty after each transaction, which in this case enabled Lindsay to make a hefty profit.

As NFTs continue to gain mainstream attention and tap into different industries, it feels like we're only scratching the surface of their potential. For sure, we can expect to see more brands experimenting different ways to harvest revenue via NFTs and engage with their fanbase/consumers. One of the current trends includes brands/people creating exclusive experiences via collectible digital assets, and then increasing its value through publicized scarcity.

Source: https://www.totalmedia.co.uk/why-nfts-will-form-part-of-your-brand-marketing-strategy-in-the-near-future/

This 12-year-old coder helped develop an NFT collection that made over $5 million in 3 weeks

Though he is just 12 years old, Benyamin Ahmed has made a name for himself in the NFT, or nonfungible token, space.

This summer, Ahmed launched two NFT projects, including Weird Whales, which earned him around $400,000 in just two months.

Around the same time, he also partnered with the developers behind Boring Bananas Co. to create Non-Fungible Heroes, an NFT collection of 8,888 comic book-esque characters.

The collection launched on Sept. 18 and sold out in just 12 minutes. To date, it has generated over $5 million in total sales, according to crypto data platform Dune Analytics.

"It was a crazy adrenaline rush. You really never know how popular your product is until you let the public at it," Ahmed says.

NFTs are unique digital assets, including jpegs and video clips, that are represented by code on a decentralized digital ledger called a blockchain. Each NFT can be bought and sold, just like physical assets, but the blockchain allows for the ownership and validity of each to be tracked.

The characters in the Non-Fungible Heroes, or NFH, universe consist of heroes, villains and gods with their own story lines. They were designed by former Disney, Marvel and Nickelodeon artists who are now part of the NFH team,

Source: https://www.cnbc.com/2021/10/01/12-year-old-helped-code-non-fungible-heroes-nfts-that-made-millions.html

Non-fungible tokens and cars - an introduction to NFTs for gearheads

The latest cryptocurrency related buzzword making millionaires out of thin air are non-fungible tokens (NFTs). These digital magic beans may be the future of classic car collecting and memorabilia, so it's worth wrapping your head around them while they're still new to take advantage of NFT related opportunities as they pop up. A simple way to think of NFTs are as certificates of authenticity for anything digital. The transaction of an NFT is recorded on something called a blockchain. The blockchain is a big list of transactions that everyone can see and provides a chain of ownership that's indisputable. There are many different blockchains around but most NFTs use the Ethereum blockchain. The NFTs themselves are traded for cryptocurrency, also typically Ethereum (aka ETH), that you buy with "real" money like Australian dollars. The NFT and cryptocurrency are stored in digital wallets that are usually smartphone apps or a website you log-in to, like Metamask or Coinbase.

Michael "Gup" Gilbert, founder of Powercruise car shows and commercially involved in Blockstar Technologies, is one of the few people with experience regarding car related NFTs, having recently purchased an NFT of a Phase III GTHO Ford Falcon for $51,000. A big reason for Gup's high purchase price of the NFT were the perks that come with it. "I do a fair bit of business with Lloyd's Auctions, so the offer of free buyer's premium and free commission on anything I buy or sell through Lloyd's was attractive to me". Gup was also keen on the potential resale value of the Phase III NFT, "I get 10% of every resale of the NFT forever, and forever is a long time".

Gup's digital Phase III also includes licensing rights to the 8TB 3D model of the classic car, but even he admits future licensing opportunities could be slim. "What are they gonna do with it? Who knows?". As for his own plans for the NFT, "I don't know what I'm going to do with it. I don't even understand where the the art portion of this purchase may take me. Maybe I'll keep it forever, maybe I won't". It's not hard to imagine car brands jumping on this opportunity to cash in on their legacies using NFTs in the near future. Ferrari making a set of NFT trading cards for all their current and past vehicles giving Ferrari a 10 per cent cut on each time they're traded. One thing is for sure, the hype around NFTs isn't going away any time soon.

Source: https://www.whichcar.com.au/news/nft-explainer

Glenfiddich Sells $18,000 Super-Rare Whisky As NFTs – Here's What That Means

There's been a lot of excitement about NFTs recently. "Non-fungible Tokens" are essentially digital code that lives on a blockchain and can be used for many purposes that relate to trust – such as proving ownership or authenticity.

We've mostly seen them used to prove ownership of digital goods – most commonly pictures but also video clips, sounds, and even tweets. Similar to what happened with Bitcoin, they evolved from a novel solution to a techy problem into a mainstream news item due to money becoming involved. A piece of art created by the artist Mike Winkelmann (known as Beeple) sold for $69 million at auction this year.

But the technology can, in theory, be used to establish ownership and provenance of just about anything. Distillers William Grant and Son have recently sold 15 bottles of 46-year-old Glenfiddich whisky for $18,000 apiece, each one accompanied by its own NFT revolving image/ artistic impression of the bottle that not only allows them to show off their purchase but also acts as a counterfeit-proof certificate of ownership. Speaking to them -as well as cousins Dov and Sam Fallic, founders of BlockBar, which handled the technical side of the project – I learned that this would be similar to the asking price for the whisky if it had been sold by traditional methods. After all, there aren't many bottles of 46-year-old whisky available, and the market for rare spirits as an investment vehicle has grown considerably in recent years.

However, launching as an NFT-backed product drew interest from a far larger pool of prospective buyers than is usually attracted to this asset class – with all 15 bottles selling in seconds. *"When we told our fathers about [NFTs], they thought we were crazy initially,"* Dov Fallic tells me. *"Who cares about something that's digital? But the younger generation spends more time in the digital world than the physical world. That's where they live, and that's where they interact."*

Source: https://www.forbes.com/sites/bernardmarr/2021/10/27/glenfiddich-sells-18000-super-rare-whisky-as-nfts--heres-what-that-means/?sh=1309da0216b8

Paris Hilton Lists a Few Pieces from Her NFT Collection via Sotheby's Metaverse Marketplace

Leading Auction House Sotheby's Introduces Metaverse NFT Market

The British-founded American multinational luxury auction headquartered in New York City, Sotheby's has been going big on non-fungible token (NFT) collectibles in recent times. Last week the company introduced the "Sotheby's Metaverse" in order to host and auction the hottest NFTs in the space. The original Sotheby's website could not offer the same experiences Metaverse offers and people can host their NFT collections by connecting with Sotheby's.

Paris Hilton Lists Her NFTs Using Sotheby's Market

On October 19, just before bitcoin (BTC) surpassed its all-time price high, the media personality, socialite, businesswoman, model, singer, and actress Paris Hilton tweeted about her new listing in the Sotheby's Metaverse NFT marketplace. "I love the amazing [artwork] for my [Natively Digital] @Sothebys @Sothebysverse Auction," Hilton said on Twitter.

Hilton's NFT collection hosted on Sotheby's Metaverse features artwork from Maalavidaa in a piece called "Fractures." Another piece by Serwah Attafuah called "Aether: Galaxy Goddess" and an NFT crafted by Chelsea Evenstar called "AQUARIUS – Keeper of the Amethyst Star."

The NFT auction listing on Sotheby's market notes that Hilton developed her first NFT in March 2020, and she won the "Best Charity NFT" at the NFT Awards ceremony. "Paris sees the NFT art market as the future, and loves that artist are pushing boundaries and changing the art industry forever," the Sotheby's listing says. It's been known for a long time that Paris Hilton is a fan of the cryptocurrency and blockchain industry as she said this past spring that she is "very, very excited" about bitcoin.

Source: https://news.bitcoin.com/paris-hilton-lists-a-few-pieces-from-her-nft-collection-via-sothebys-metaverse-marketplace/

Disney to Drop 'Golden Moments' NFT Collectible Series via Digital Collectibles App Veve

Disney has plans to launch official non-fungible token (NFT) collectibles in celebration of the first annual Disney+ Day. The well-known multinational entertainment and media conglomerate headquartered in California has revealed a series of NFTs featuring iconic Disney characters and items.

The first series collection is called "Golden Moments," and fans will be able to obtain the NFTs by utilizing the digital collectibles app Veve. The Veve application has dropped NFTs stemming from Marvel, DC Comics, and special promotions based on beloved superheroes like Spider-Man and Captain America.

The "Golden Moments" Disney NFT series will feature "digital golden statues inspired by beloved stories and moments from Disney, Pixar, Marvel, [and] Star Wars." According to Veve, the new Disney NFTs will soon be available via the app and will "culminate on Disney+ Day on November 12."

On that day, a "special Ultra Rare digital collectible" will be introduced as well. Veve says the drop dates will be revealed ahead of time and if a customer purchases an NFT from the "Golden Moments" collection, they will get three months of Disney+ TV from Veve.

Veve Technology Claims to Offer 'Gasless Transactions'

The Disney+ promo is available in the United States, Canada, United Kingdom, Germany, Australia, Netherlands, Spain, Mexico, and Singapore. However, the Disney+ TV subscription offer doesn't apply to secondary NFT sales.

Information regarding the Disney "Golden Moments" NFT collectibles series can be found on Veve's web portal. Veve says the application they offer leverages "an augmented reality (AR) photo mode" which allows collectors to interact with the NFT.

According to Veve, the technology used to mint the non-fungible token collectibles it offers utilizes "gasless transactions providing a 99.9% reduction in environmental footprint."

Source: https://news.bitcoin.com/disney-to-drop-golden-moments-nft-collectible-series-via-digital-collectibles-app-veve/

How NFTs are empowering recording artists and helping them escape centralized platforms

Nonfungible tokens, or NFTs, allow independent artists to earn income and engage with their fan base without having to always rely on a label or streaming service like Spotify. In March, 3LAU, an electronic dance music producer, sold more than $11 million worth of tokens redeemable for real-world goods — including music — in addition to a $3 million token holder who bid for the right to collaborate with the artist. Paul Oakenfold, another well-known EDM DJ, announced in September he would be launching a tokenized album on the Cardano blockchain.

Many venues around the world are still unable to hold live concerts due to restrictions brought on by the pandemic, and some streaming services do not offer a sustainable income for artists. Rather than shirking COVID-19 guidelines, some performers and organizers have turned to blockchain technology in the form of metaverses and NFTs for alternative solutions. In August, Epic Games' Fortnite hosted a virtual concert with singer Ariana Grande and others.

One project claims to be revolutionizing the music space, offering music fans creative access to top artists, while wetting the palette of blockchain newbies and veterans through the merging of blockchain technology with mainstream entertainment. Animal Concerts' fans can go to live or virtual concerts, while also retaining some control of their own content with the platform's utility tokens. NFTs also play a large role and are used for virtual venue tickets, future live events, avatars for fans and souvenirs for certain performances.

"We are at the apex of several emerging technologies, streaming, VR, metaverses and NFTs and well-positioned to capitalize on this as the only one bringing it all together in one place," said Animal Concerts CEO Colin Fitzpatrick. "For musicians, this is the first new major revenue stream in a decade and an exciting and innovative way to interact with their fans. We're democratizing concerts and bringing the power directly back to the artists themselves."

Source: https://cointelegraph.com/news/how-nfts-are-empowering-recording-artists-and-helping-them-escape-centralized-platforms

Conclusion

What is the secret behind NFT's success?

NFT Marketing, of course.

The growing popularity of NFT alongside the increasing number of NFT marketplaces means everyone is getting in on that trend.

The NFT industry is a hot topic that never seems to fade away. Every day, we see more people joining the craze and following this trending sensation in art form--from music tracks or games themselves!

Artists everywhere are making significant revenue by selling their unique content on these marketplaces where buyers can purchase pieces at affordable prices with ease thanks also having to access to them anytime, they want through digitalization technology like blockchain which allows you full ownership of what was once yours alone

The secret behind NFT's success can be attributed to how it has been marketed.

The growing popularity of these NFT/tokens alongside the increasing number of marketplaces means everyone is getting in on that trend, which means more artists want their content to stand out from others and earn revenue by creating unique merchandise with cryptocurrency as payment options.

Plans must include:

- Pre & Post Promoting
- Community Building
- Story Branding
- Creative Graphic (brand build, art)
- Social Media
- FOMO Demand
- Gateway Marketing: Discord, Telegram, Twitter
- Roadmap, Giveaways, Promotions beyond the purchase
- Community Relations
- Influencer Marketing
- PR Marketing
- Search Engine Marketing
- Paid Advertising

Interested in more information?

Schedule an NFT Strategy session with me:

www.AndyBroadaway.com

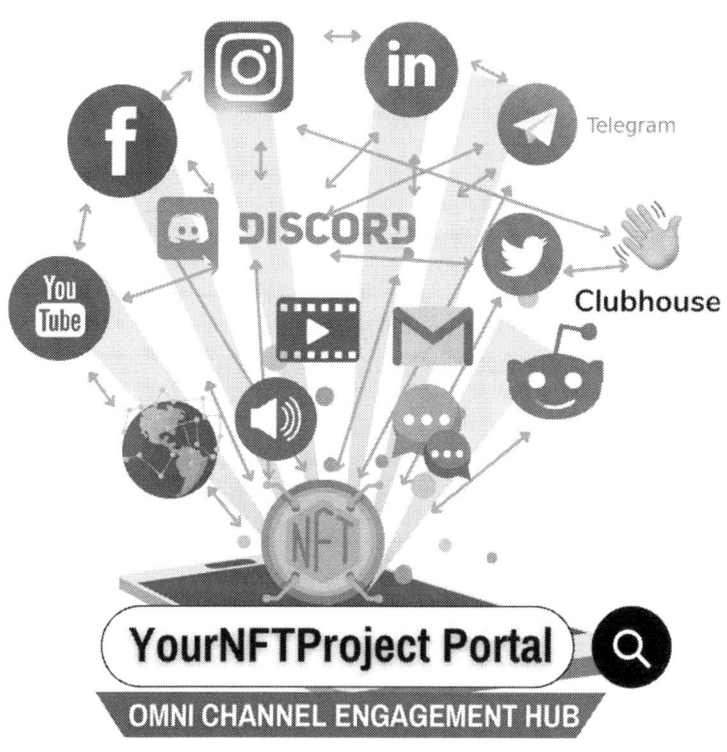

NFT Business Uses & Project Ideas

- Artwork / Gifs / JPG / Animation
- Music/ Video
- Gaming
- Rewards Programs
- Concerts/Events
- Experiences
- Non-Physical/Physical Goods
- Books
- Educational portal
- Real estate
- Online Communities
- Charity
- IP/Domains/Trademarks
- Smart Contracts / Certifications
- Restaurant
- Investment Firm / Portfolio

Glossary of Terms

1/1 — *A "one of one" or "1/1" is a unique piece of art. A "1/1" can be a standalone NFT (e.g., a unique creation by a digital artist), or it can also be a super rare 1/1 inserted into a larger generative set. (Although, technically, all items within a larger generative set are generally also unique. We just don't usually call normal members of generative sets 1/1s.)*

Ape — *This term, often used as a verb, is particular to the NFT world. It refers to the Bored Ape Yacht Club, one of the blue chip OG generative NFT sets (arguably the gold standard among NFT drops, with top-quality, whimsical generative art and insanely high values per NFT). People use the term in different ways. As a verb — to ape, or to ape into — it can mean "to buy," "to buy in early," "to rise in value." But, it's flexible, too. One might say, "Wow, that's gonna be an ape-level drop!"*

Assets – *this is just an industry term for a digital collectible – it could be a model, piece of art, music, a tweet or anything else you can buy as an NFT. Not everyone will call items assets, but it's useful to know in case it does pop up in conversation.*

2D/3D – *You already know what these terms are and might be wondering what they have to do with NFTs and crypto, but basically it describes the kind of item you are buying; 2D would be something like a poster, 3D would be a digital model. Here's an example of a 2D collectible, and a 3D collectible.*

2DA/3D – *This means 2D Animated or 3D Animated. You've probably guessed that these are animated versions of 3D models or 2D artwork. Basically, there's something in the collectible that will move. If it's a 2D Animated picture, you might find that the background moves, or that snow is falling. For a 3D Animated* model (such as our Godzilla models) they will actually move around with cool actions – pretty neat, right!

Bitcoin – *The cryptocurrency that started all the hype. This is the most well-known cryptocurrency. The original purpose of Bitcoin was as an alternative payment method that would bypass banks and regular financial institutions, and there are plenty of retailers who will accept Bitcoin as payment for everyday goods and services. However these days most people are buying cryptocurrency as a form of investment, due to its rising value.*

Blockchain – *This is the basis of all cryptocurrencies and NFTs. It was conceived by Satoshi Nakamoto in 2008 as a decentralized (i.e. not controlled by one person, company, or entity) leger of transactions. In short, it's a way of keeping track of all transactions that occur within the blockchain, and there are also protocols set up to validate these transactions, so you know that what you're buying, sending, or receiving is authentic.*

Burning – *Another cryptocurrency term; burning means permanently deleting or eliminating a specific amount of a cryptocurrency. It's done for a number of reasons; it can be used as part of the blockchain authentication process (via something called Proof-of-Burning), or it can be used to moderate the value of a cryptocurrency (if there are fewer in circulation, the value goes up). Again, this is quite a technical term, so just one to be aware of unless you're eager to get into this in a deep way.*

Crypto – *This has become the de facto term for anything to do with cryptocurrencies, NFTs, digital collectibles etc. It's a catch-all word, so does get used in a variety of ways, so be careful not to assume that someone is using it in the same way you do.*

Cryptocurrency – *You've probably heard of cryptocurrencies such as Bitcoin and Ethereum, and maybe even Ripple (and hopefully Terra Virtua Kolect a.k.a TVK, which is our cryptocurrency token).*

In the pure sense, these are digital currencies (i.e. payment methods) that you can use to buy things on the blockchain. However, again be wary of how people are using the term as it does get thrown about and used incorrectly.

Discord - *Discord is a VoIP, instant messaging and digital distribution platform. Users communicate with voice calls, video calls, text messaging, media and files in private chats or as part of communities called "servers". Servers are a collection of persistent chat rooms and voice chat channels. Discord runs on Windows, macOS, Android, iOS, iPadOS, Linux, and in web browsers. As of 2021, the service has over 350 million registered users and over 150 million monthly active users.*

DeFi – *This is shorthand for Decentralised Finance, which is a catch-all term for any kind of financial activity that uses cryptocurrency and blockchain principles. You probably won't come across this one a lot, but again it's useful to know, as it's a growing field and will be popping up more and more in everyday discussions.*

Diamondhands — *These are the NFT owners who hold for the long term. They're in it for the long-haul and believe in the massive payout ahead.*

Digital collectibles – *Our favorite term! In short, this is a brand new way to celebrate your fandom for your favorite films, TV, bands, sports, everything basically. Instead (or as well) of collecting physical items that you probably don't use (or even take out of the packet) you can fill your boots with digital toys, posters, and more that you can enjoy and interact with. We've got loads of great resources to help explain this one, so check out our blog and intro video for examples and fun ideas.*

Drop – *If you're following us on social media, or part of our Discord or Telegram communities you will probably see us talking about 'drops'. This is just the term we use for the release of new digital collectibles. So if something is 'dropping' at 5 pm, it means that's when you can hop online and buy it.*

DYOR — *Do Your Own Research. Just because someone you know and maybe even respect says to buy, that doesn't mean that you should do so. Don't blindly follow anyone in the NFT space. (Well, okay, unless GaryVee says to buy, in which case a set's gonna sell out. lol, jk.)*

Ethereum – *This one is actually a bit confusing because Ethereum is talked about as both an exchange platform (i.e. you can trade things using the Ethereum platform, which is what we use at Terra Virtua) and a cryptocurrency. However, the official currency name is Eth, so if you want to buy the cryptocurrency, just bear that in mind.*

Exchange – *Similar to the old-school stock exchange, this is a place to buy and sell cryptocurrencies. There are a few around, some more reputable than others, so if you are considering getting into the cryptocurrency game please do your research and don't just go with any old exchange.*

Farm – *This relates to the mining of cryptocurrency. Farms are large-scale operations that make mining more efficient.*

Floor — *The floor, or floor price, is the lowest price that an NFT (usually within a larger set) can be purchased. NFT buyers watch the floor like hawks, and it's common to have dedicated channels within project Discords devoted to analyzing the floor — why it's where it is, where it's going, where it was before, etc. People talk about the floor price in general, and they also talk about the floor of subsets of a drop. For example, the floor price today for the*

Bored Apes is 34 ETH. But the floor price for a "Trippy"-furred ape is 175 ETH.

FOMO — *Fear Of Missing Out. This is a psychological phenomenon that kicks in at various times and influences buyer behavior. It's often used as a verb: "Oh, you FOMO'd into that one!" In the NFT world, just think of it as making a purchase out of fear that a project will moon (see below) and you'll miss out on the rewards.*

Fren — *Friend. One of a handful of common child-like spellings you'll see. Usage of these types of words is super common in the NFT space. But, I have to admit that, as a writer, I'm not a giant fan of these words.*

FUD — *Fear, Uncertainty, Doubt. It's everywhere, often spread purposely by those looking to troll an NFT drop or market for some reason. I've seen this get really ugly and takeover an otherwise healthy discussion, and even more or less ruin a drop. The best way to prevent and/or quiet FUD is via active mods in your Discord, and of course by attracting positive community members.*

Fiat – *Not the little car, this type of fiat actually just means money. Technically it means any currency that a government has confirmed as legal tender, and is backed by the government that has issued it. So, yeah, it's just a fancy term for everyday money but is a useful way to distinguish between normal currencies and digital ones.*

Gamification - *is the strategic attempt to enhance systems, services, organizations, and activities in order to create similar experiences to those experienced when playing games in order to motivate and engage users. This is generally accomplished through the application of game-design elements and game principles (dynamics and mechanics) in non-game contexts. It can also be defined as a set of activities and processes to solve problems by using or applying the characteristics of game elements.*

Gamification is part of persuasive system design, and it commonly employs game design elements to improve user engagement, organizational productivity, crowdsourcing, knowledge retention, employee recruitment and evaluation, ease of use, the usefulness of systems, physical exercise, traffic violations, voter apathy, public attitudes about alternative energy, and more. A collection of research on gamification shows that a majority of studies on gamification find it has positive effects on individuals. However, individual and contextual differences exist.

Gas – *Another technical term, that's a bit complex, but essentially this is the 'fee' you have to pay to transact something on the Ethereum blockchain. The price of gas is set by the miners on the blockchain and can rise and fall depending on supply and demand. This affects you if you are minting (definition below) items for sale or buying items using the Ethereum network or Eth currency.*

Generative Set — *A generative NFT set is one in which the images are programmatically generated. Again, see the Bored Ape Yacht Club for a typical example. Typically, these sets contain various asset classes (in the case of Bored Apes, it's Backgrounds, Clothes, Earrings, Eyes, Fur, Hats, and Mouths). Within each asset class there are numerous traits, some of which are rarer than others. In the case of the Bored Apes there are 8 different Backgrounds, 43 different Clothes, 6 different Earrings, 23 different Eyes, 19 different Fur styles, 36 different Hats, and 33 different Mouths. Those are then run through an algorithm to produce unique permutations from the above list, based on what's called a rarity table (which controls the distribution of traits)*

Hashmask – *A kind of artwork, normally created by multiple artists in collaboration. The special part of hashmasks is that when you buy one, you can actually choose the name yourself, which is unusual for an NFT, so adds additional value to the item.*

HODL – *Also written in lowercase as hodl, this is a misspelling of the word HOLD (i.e. keep hold of your cryptocurrencies rather than selling them off), which became a meme and is now a standard term in the crypto-verse.*

Key – *Core to the security of cryptocurrencies and digital trading, your key is sort of like a password, but is auto-generated and links your account to the blockchain. When you register for any kind of crypto-based activity you get two keys: public and private. The public key traces the transaction on the blockchain, the private key is unique to you and secures your account. Top tip: do not lose your private key as it cannot be recovered and without it, you can't access your account.*

Metadata — *An NFTs metadata is what describes the properties of the NFT, including the image itself. For example, here's the metadata for Bored Ape #1. You can see that it points to the IPFS for the image (here) and that it's got a grin, Vietnam jacket, orange background, blue beam eyes, and robot fur (and all of that matches up with the image). Sites like OpenSea use the metadata to be able to allow users to filter collections. (For example, to see all apes with "Blue Beams" eyes, go here.)*

Metamask – *Metamask is a third-party crypto-wallet that Terra Virtua utilizes. You can always link your Metamask account with your Terra Virtua account. There are other wallets, but not everything is co-compatible, so always check the requirements of the wallets, marketplaces, and exchanges you are using.*

Mining – *The process of obtaining small bits of cryptocurrencies and adding them to the blockchain. Miners use complicated computer methods to verify and validate transactions, add these to the blockchain and let others on the network know that something has been added. If you're a miner you can keep hold of these for yourself or sell them on.*

Minted – *This is the process of validating information and adding that to the blockchain. This is a core part of NFTs, and what makes them so valuable, because once an item or asset is minted, this is proof that it's authentic, and keeps track of how many there are. On the Terra Virtua marketplace, for example, on all items, you'll see info on how many were minted and which number you are buying. This allows you to prove that you have an authentic item, and one of only a few in existence. Minting is done by computers connected to the blockchain, so it's not something you'll probably have to deal with from a technical standpoint, but understanding what minting means, will allow you to feel confident you're buying genuine products.*

Moon — *To moon is a verb. It means to hit that ever-elusive valuation for an NFT that everyone hopes for. With their 34 ETH floor, Bored Apes definitely mooned. For other projects, the term may be more subjective. Pudgy Penguins has a 1.28 floor. Did it moon? Kinda-sorta. Cool Cats has a 5.8 ETH floor. Did that one moon? Sure, I'd say so. Can a project that already mooned moon again?*

NFT – *Shorthand for Non-fungible token. What this means is that it cannot be replaced by an identical item. So basically all NFTs are unique. Now, that doesn't mean that there's only one piece of artwork, etc., but there is only one with that unique blockchain data. Note that a token can be applied to anything, an image, a 3D model, music, anything in the digital realm basically.*

Noob – *Nickname for someone new to the crypto space. If that's you, welcome, we're excited to be your part of this great community!*

Rarities – *As the term implies this is all about how rare an NFT is. For some NFTs there are thousands available to buy, hence they're viewed as a low rarity. If, however, there is just one of an NFT* *minted on the blockchain, then it's super rare, and therefore more valuable. There's no common lexicon for different rarities, at Terra Virtua we have a rating system for how rare our assets are, but each platform will have different categories and criteria, so always check before you buy to make sure you're paying a fair price for a specified rarity.*

Staking – *When you 'stake' a cryptocurrency, you are adding your crypto to a collaborative wallet, to allow proof-of-staking activities to take place. There's more on the technical side but at a top-level, it means temporarily locking your cryptocurrency into that wallet, so you can't access or spend it. However, it's a popular use of cryptocurrencies, as typically you'll gain rewards for being part of the staking community, so it can be quite beneficial depending on the currency. It's also growing in popularity as proof-of-staking is a more efficient way to authenticate blockchain transactions. You will soon be able to stake your TVK with Terra Virtua via our Prestige Programme, which will give you access to all kinds of cool rewards. Keep an eye on social media for more info on this.*

Paperhands — *These are the people who buy into an NFT project, but then sell too quickly — either taking a minimal gain or possibly even a loss because they may be nervous about the project being a rug, or because of online FUD being spread.*

PFP — *Sometimes "picture for proof," but I usually think "profile pic" (the latter being more common, but perhaps making less sense as an acronym). It's a common style of NFT drop, typically in the generative set world, in which the NFTs feature a character, usually facing forward, suitable for use online as an avatar.*

Prereveal — *During an NFT drop, there's quite often a span of time between when the sale happens and when the final images actually show up on OpenSea. This is the "prereveal" period. During this time, a prereveal image (think of it as a temporary image) shows* when users go to their wallets and take a look (e.g., when they login to OpenSea and look at their profiles, which shows what they just bought). Drops generally do this on purpose, and for a few reasons. First, if the drop were to show the actual images upon purchase, savvy users could potentially look ahead at the set's metadata and know when super rare items were coming, and then snipe them. At least, that was the initial purpose of prerevealing.

But there's more to it. Allowing the metadata to be seen prior to a sale's end opens up the world to fraud (as bots could collect all images and metadata from the set and easily launch a copy of the set as a scam). Also, the practice has evolved now into a whole other market-run phenomenon, which is the prereveal secondary market — that period of time between the primary sale and the reveal during which speculators often run the price up in a frenzy.

Presale — The presale is a part of the primary sale, generally a time set aside for early adopters and other whitelisted people to come to a mint page and purchase NFTs. It's done both as a courtesy, a reward or thank-you gesture (to ensure that these people actually get NFTs — which may not be otherwise guaranteed in the case of a massively popular drop), and/or simply as a measure to mitigate gas wars.

Primary Sale — The primary sale is the initial sale period of an NFT drop. This typically takes place at a minting page on the drop's web site.

Reveal — Technically speaking, the "reveal" is when a drop changes the metadata pointer on their smart contract, which has the effect of changing the images for an NFT set (thus finally revealing the actual image and property data after a prereveal period). It's always a fun time, and a good time to be in a drop's Discord to watch the reactions.

Roadmap — *The roadmap has become an essential element of an NFT drop's existence. Basically, this outlines what's going to happen down the line for a project. In the early days, before 10-minute sellouts were much of a thing, it was typical to see roadmaps that said things like "At 10% sales, we're going to do X. At 25% sales, we're going to do Y. At 50% sales, we're going to do Z." But I sense that sort of thing is going away for a few reasons.*

First, nowadays, a sale can sell out in minutes or hours, and thus it's pointless to set yourself up to do some huge activity at 10% sold, and then another at 20% sold. You're not going to launch at noon, hire a developer to start sketching out a video game at 12:15 p.m., and then have that game in beta testing by 1:00 p.m. And furthermore, the NFT space has unfortunately evolved into such an investment-centric world that, if a project does not sell out in a day, it becomes a massive perception issue.

That all said, while you probably don't need the "10%, 20%, 30%" style roadmap, you likely DO want some sort of plan showing what you're going to do — both with funds generated and just in general as time goes on. I'll say also that, quite commonly these days there's some sort of charitable component to NFT drops. (One of our own clients has one coming up for which he's donating a whopping 70% of the primary sale to charity!)

Rug — *This is when a drop team "pulls the rug out" on a project. For example, maybe they promised all sorts of great developments, activities, and community benefits post-drop but, after the ETH rolled in, they just took the ETH and ran. That would be a rug. They rugged the project. You got rugged. Not good. Sadly common.*

Secondary Market — *This is all of the buying and selling that goes on after the primary sale. Basically, this is everything you see, all of the trading, going on with generative sets on Opensea.*

The Bored Apes have done 200k ETH in secondary market activity. That's $900+ million.

Sellout — Ha, and you thought this term was only for rock-and-roll bands who went mainstream? Nah, it means that a generative NFT set has sold out, indicating a massive success. And btw, this can happen in minutes, hours, days, weeks, or longer. In my book, a sellout is a sellout. There's no shame in a drop making $2 million in months versus minutes, though the market may say otherwise.

Smart Contract — The smart contract is the code that lives on the blockchain and governs the NFT sale — allowing for certain functionality such as minting — and keeps various other important information such as the metadata address for the NFTs. The code is unchangeable once deployed, although some things (if coded for) can be updated via interactions with the contract.

Sweep the Floor — To sweep the floor is to purchase NFTs from a set at floor price. This is often done by investors who believe in a project and wish to purchase additional NFTs from a set while also helping to raise the floor price (because, if they and others buy up the lowest-price NFTs, the floor price naturally rises, which can positively affect the perception of value a set has).

Tokenomics – Simply the term for the economics of cryptocurrencies. It comes from combining 'token' and 'economics', clever eh? It's an interesting area to look into, and well worth exploring if you'd like to learn more about how cryptocurrencies behave, for example, what makes prices rise and fall, and why certain tokens are more valuable than others.

Utility Token — Some NFTs are not merely JPGs (or PNGs, as the case may be). Some have utility, such as granting digital access to web sites or Discord groups, or even real-life access to events. (VeeFriends does this a lot.)

Verified Contract — *"Verified" does not necessarily mean "good" like it sounds. But, a verified contract is one where you can actually read, study, and audit, the code, thus making it considerably safer to trust, as it's now auditable by third-parties. It seems like months ago, having a verified contract publicly available was a must for drops. And I still think savvy investors like this. But, some drops are choosing not to verify, ostensibly for security reasons. I believe MekaVerse did not verify (at least not during their primary sale). That said, I recommend drops verify pre-sale and make the contract available for inspection.*

Wen — *When. It's common for people to ask "wen moon?" ("When will this NFT set skyrocket in value?") or "web lambo?" ("When will I be able to sell this NFT and afford a Lamborghini?"). See my comments on "fren" above.*

WGMI — *We're Gonna Make It. Well, unless you aren't, in which cast you're NGMI (though I haven't included that one here).*

Whitelist — *A whitelist is a group of wallet or email addresses to which access is granted to a presale. People love to ape in early, get on the whitelist, mint their tokens, and hope they moon.*

Wallet – *You already know what a wallet is in the real world, and it's basically the same in crypto land. It's a place to hold your cryptocurrencies. Simple. And when you add a wallet to a store or exchange, you can buy NFTs, and trade cryptocurrencies. Again, there are a lot of wallets out there, so do some research before you settle on the one that's right for you.*

Made in the USA
Monee, IL
08 February 2022

20f3e775-1ced-4ab2-917e-52f89b641d10R01